Hungary

Everything You Need to Know

Copyright © 2024 by Noah Gil-Smith.

All rights reserved. No part of this book may be reproduced, distributed, or transmitted in any form or by any means, including photocopying, recording, or other electronic or mechanical methods, without the prior written permission of the publisher, except in the case of brief quotations embodied in critical reviews and certain other noncommercial uses permitted by copyright law. This book was created with the assistance of Artificial Intelligence. The content presented in this book is for entertainment purposes only. It should not be considered as a substitute for professional advice or comprehensive research. Readers are encouraged to independently verify any information and consult relevant experts for specific matters. The author and publisher disclaim any liability or responsibility for any loss, injury, or inconvenience caused or alleged to be caused directly or indirectly by the information presented in this book.

Introduction to Hungary 6

The Geographical Tapestry: Exploring Hungary's Diverse Landscape 9

Tracing Hungary's Origins: From Ancient Times to the Birth of a Nation 11

Medieval Hungary: Kingdoms, Conquests, and Cultural Flourishes 14

Ottoman Rule and Habsburg Influence: Shaping Hungary's Destiny 17

Revolution and Independence: The Struggle for Sovereignty 20

The World Wars and Hungary's Turbulent 20th Century 23

Post-Communist Era: Transition and Transformation 27

Budapest: Jewel of the Danube 30

Exploring Historic Treasures: Must-See Sites in Budapest 33

Beyond Budapest: Exploring Hungary's Other Major Cities 35

Pécs: A Journey Through History and Culture 37

Debrecen: Gateway to the Great Hungarian Plain 39

Szeged: Where Tradition Meets Innovation 42

Cultural Identity: Hungarian Folklore and Traditions 45

Festivals and Celebrations: A Calendar of Hungarian Culture 48

The Puszta: Exploring Hungary's Great Plain and Wildlife 51

Danube Delta: Nature's Splendor Along Hungary's Waterways 54

Hungarian Vineyards and Wines: A Toast to Tradition 56

Architectural Marvels: From Castles to Thermal Baths 58

The Legacy of the Austro-Hungarian Empire: Art, Architecture, and Influence 61

Music and Dance: The Heartbeat of Hungarian Culture 63

Hungarian Literature: From Epic Poetry to Contemporary Prose 66

Religion in Hungary: Faith and Heritage 69

Education and Intellectual Heritage: Hungary's Scholarly Legacy 71

The Hungarian Language: An Introduction and Overview 74

Hungarian Etiquette and Social Customs: Navigating Cultural Norms 76

Folk Art and Crafts: Preserving Tradition in a Modern World 78

Hungarian Fashion and Design: A Blend of Tradition and Innovation 80

Sports and Recreation: From Football to Water Polo 82

Health and Wellness: Hungary's Thermal Spa Culture 84

Transportation in Hungary: Navigating Roads, Rails, and Rivers 86

Economy and Industry: Hungary's Economic Landscape 88

Environmental Concerns and Conservation Efforts 91

Minority Cultures in Hungary: Preserving Diversity 93

Immigration and Diaspora: Hungarian Communities Around the World 95

Government and Politics: Structure and Challenges 97

Hungarian Diplomacy: Navigating International Relations 99

Tourism in Hungary: Opportunities and Challenges 101

Cultural Exchange and Collaboration: Hungary on the Global Stage 103

Future Prospects: Challenges and Opportunities for Hungary 105

Epilogue 108

Introduction to Hungary

Hungary, a land of rich history, vibrant culture, and captivating landscapes, beckons travelers with its allure. Nestled in the heart of Central Europe, bordered by seven countries, this enchanting nation has been a crossroads of civilizations for centuries. Its strategic location along the Danube River has shaped its destiny, molding a heritage that is both diverse and distinctive.

Stretching over 93,000 square kilometers, Hungary's geography is as varied as it is picturesque. From the rolling hills of Transdanubia to the vast plains of the Great Hungarian Plain, every corner of the country tells a story of its own. The Carpathian Mountains cradle the northern border, offering stunning vistas and outdoor adventures for the intrepid explorer. Meanwhile, the Great Hungarian Plain, or the Puszta, unfolds across the southeastern reaches, showcasing endless plains dotted with grazing livestock and traditional horsemen.

But it's not just the landscape that captivates; Hungary's history is a tapestry woven with threads of triumph and turmoil. Its roots can be traced back to ancient times, with evidence of human settlement dating back to the Paleolithic era. Over the millennia, Hungary has witnessed the rise and fall of empires, from the Celtic and Roman influences to the Magyar conquest in the 9th century, which laid the foundation for the Hungarian nation.

The medieval era saw Hungary emerge as a regional powerhouse under the rule of the Árpád dynasty. Budapest, its capital, grew into a vibrant center of commerce and culture, earning the title "Queen of the Danube." Yet, Hungary's fortunes took a dramatic turn with the arrival of the Ottoman Turks in the 16th century, ushering in a period of foreign occupation and strife.

The 19th century brought renewed hope for independence, culminating in the 1848 Revolution and War of Independence. Although initially suppressed, the seeds of nationalism had been sown, leading to the eventual collapse of the Austro-Hungarian Empire in the aftermath of World War I. The Treaty of Trianon in 1920, however, dealt a devastating blow to Hungary, stripping away two-thirds of its territory and leaving millions of ethnic Hungarians outside its borders.

The tumultuous 20th century brought further challenges, from the horrors of World War II to the stifling grip of communist rule under Soviet influence. Hungary's journey to democracy and independence was marked by struggle and sacrifice, culminating in the fall of the Iron Curtain in 1989 and the subsequent transition to a democratic republic.

Today, Hungary stands at a crossroads, balancing its rich heritage with the demands of modernity. Its bustling cities pulse with energy, blending historic charm with contemporary flair. Budapest, with its stunning architecture, thermal baths, and vibrant nightlife, remains a perennial favorite among travelers. Beyond the capital, a treasure trove of cultural gems awaits discovery, from the medieval town of Pécs to the picturesque vineyards of Tokaj.

As Hungary charts its course in the 21st century, it continues to captivate visitors with its timeless allure. Whether wandering the cobblestone streets of Eger or savoring a traditional goulash in a rustic tavern, each moment spent in Hungary is an invitation to delve deeper into its rich tapestry of history, culture, and natural beauty.

The Geographical Tapestry: Exploring Hungary's Diverse Landscape

Hungary's geographical tapestry is a testament to the country's diverse and captivating landscape. Nestled in the heart of Central Europe, Hungary boasts a range of topographical features that make it both unique and picturesque.

One of the defining features of Hungary's landscape is its location along the Carpathian Basin, a vast lowland surrounded by the Carpathian Mountains to the north and east, and the Dinaric Alps to the south. This basin encompasses much of Hungary's territory, providing fertile plains and valleys that have long sustained agriculture and settlement.

To the north of Hungary lies the Bükk Mountains, a scenic range characterized by rugged limestone peaks, dense forests, and cascading waterfalls. This region offers ample opportunities for outdoor recreation, including hiking, caving, and birdwatching in the Bükk National Park.

In the west, the Transdanubian Hills roll gently towards the Danube River, creating a patchwork of vineyards, orchards, and charming villages. This region is known for its wine production, particularly in areas such as the Balaton Uplands and the Villány-Siklós wine region.

The Great Hungarian Plain, or the Puszta, dominates the southeastern part of the country. This vast expanse of flatland stretches as far as the eye can see, interrupted only by occasional rivers and patches of forest. The Puszta is renowned for its pastoral landscapes and traditional Hungarian horsemen, who showcase their equestrian skills in annual festivals and exhibitions.

The Danube River, Europe's second-longest river, flows majestically through the heart of Hungary, dividing the country into two distinct regions: Transdanubia to the west and the Great Hungarian Plain to the east. The Danube not only serves as a vital transportation artery but also as a scenic backdrop for some of Hungary's most iconic landmarks, including the Parliament Building and Buda Castle in Budapest.

In addition to its natural beauty, Hungary is also home to a wealth of thermal springs and spas, thanks to its rich geological history. The city of Budapest alone boasts over 100 thermal springs, earning it the nickname "City of Spas." These mineral-rich waters have been revered for their healing properties since Roman times, attracting visitors from around the world to indulge in relaxation and rejuvenation.

From the verdant hills of the north to the sun-drenched plains of the south, Hungary's diverse landscape offers something for every traveler to discover and explore. Whether hiking in the mountains, cruising along the Danube, or soaking in a thermal bath, the beauty of Hungary's geography never fails to enchant and inspire.

Tracing Hungary's Origins: From Ancient Times to the Birth of a Nation

Tracing Hungary's origins is like embarking on an archaeological journey through the annals of time, where layers of history unveil the intricate tapestry of civilization that shaped this Central European nation. The story of Hungary's genesis begins thousands of years ago, with evidence of human habitation dating back to the Paleolithic era. Nomadic tribes roamed the fertile plains of the Carpathian Basin, leaving behind artifacts and settlements that provide glimpses into their way of life.

By the first millennium BCE, the region was inhabited by various Celtic tribes, who established fortified settlements and engaged in trade with neighboring peoples. Yet, it was the arrival of the Magyars, a nomadic people of Uralic origin, in the 9th century that would leave an indelible mark on Hungary's history. Led by Árpád, the Magyars settled in the Carpathian Basin, forming the foundation of what would later become the Hungarian nation.

Under the rule of the Árpád dynasty, Hungary began to take shape as a cohesive political entity. The Magyars, influenced by both Eastern and Western cultures, adopted Christianity and established a kingdom that encompassed much of present-day Hungary. Budapest, then known as Aquincum, emerged as a prominent center of trade and culture, serving as the capital of the Kingdom of Hungary.

Throughout the medieval period, Hungary experienced periods of expansion and consolidation, as well as conflicts with neighboring powers such as the Byzantine Empire and the Holy Roman Empire. The reign of King Stephen I, who was crowned in 1000 CE and later canonized as Saint Stephen, marked a turning point in Hungary's history. Under his rule, Christianity was firmly established as the state religion, laying the groundwork for Hungary's integration into European Christendom.

The 13th century brought new challenges with the Mongol invasion and subsequent occupation, which devastated much of Hungary and left lasting scars on the landscape. However, Hungary rebounded, and by the late Middle Ages, it had become a regional powerhouse, with a flourishing economy, vibrant culture, and significant influence in European affairs.

The Renaissance and Reformation brought both intellectual and religious ferment to Hungary, as humanist ideas spread and religious reformers challenged the authority of the Catholic Church. Yet, it was the Ottoman invasion in the 16th century that would usher in a period of profound transformation and upheaval. For over 150 years, Hungary was under Ottoman rule, enduring warfare, occupation, and cultural assimilation.

The struggle for independence reached its zenith with the Hungarian Revolution of 1848, a watershed moment in Hungary's history. Although ultimately suppressed by Austrian and Russian forces, the revolution sparked a renewed sense of national identity and paved the way for Hungary's eventual emancipation from Habsburg rule.

The late 19th and early 20th centuries witnessed Hungary's emergence as a modern nation-state, with the establishment of a parliamentary government and efforts to promote Hungarian language and culture. However, the aftermath of World War I brought territorial losses and political upheaval, as Hungary grappled with the consequences of the Treaty of Trianon and the collapse of the Austro-Hungarian Empire.

Despite the challenges of the 20th century, Hungary persevered, forging a path to democracy and independence in the aftermath of World War II and the fall of communism. Today, Hungary stands as a proud and resilient nation, its history a testament to the enduring spirit of its people and the rich tapestry of cultures that have shaped its identity over the centuries.

Medieval Hungary: Kingdoms, Conquests, and Cultural Flourishes

In the annals of Hungary's history, the medieval period stands as a testament to the country's resilience, innovation, and cultural dynamism. From the 9th to the 15th century, Hungary experienced a remarkable era of growth and transformation, marked by the rise of powerful kingdoms, the expansion of territory through conquests, and flourishing artistic and intellectual endeavors.

Under the rule of the Árpád dynasty, which began with the legendary chieftain Árpád in the late 9th century, Hungary emerged as a cohesive political entity. The Magyars, a nomadic people of Uralic origin, settled in the Carpathian Basin and established a kingdom that encompassed much of present-day Hungary. The Árpád dynasty, which lasted for over four centuries, laid the foundation for Hungary's medieval statehood and played a crucial role in shaping its identity.

During the early medieval period, Hungary experienced both internal consolidation and external expansion. Under King Stephen I, who was crowned in 1000 CE and later canonized as Saint Stephen, Hungary underwent a process of Christianization and state-building. Stephen's reign saw the adoption of Christianity as the state religion, the establishment of ecclesiastical institutions, and the introduction of feudalism, which helped centralize royal authority and solidify the kingdom's administrative structure.

Throughout the medieval era, Hungary's strategic location in Central Europe made it a key player in regional politics and warfare. The Kingdom of Hungary expanded its territory through a series of military campaigns and diplomatic alliances, extending its influence into neighboring regions such as Transylvania, Croatia, and Slavonia. The reign of King Béla IV in the 13th century witnessed the construction of numerous fortifications, including stone castles and fortified towns, to defend against foreign invasions, particularly from the Mongols and later the Ottoman Turks.

Despite the challenges of external threats and internal strife, medieval Hungary experienced a period of cultural and economic flourishing. The kingdom's vibrant cities, such as Buda, Pest, and Székesfehérvár, became centers of trade, commerce, and culture, attracting merchants, artisans, and intellectuals from across Europe. Hungarian kings and nobles patronized the arts, commissioning illuminated manuscripts, religious artworks, and architectural marvels that reflected the diverse influences of Romanesque, Gothic, and Renaissance styles.

The medieval period also witnessed the emergence of Hungarian literature, with the epic poem "Gesta Hungarorum" attributed to the chronicler Anonymus, and the "Chronicle of Buda" by János Thuróczi, providing valuable insights into Hungary's early history and folklore. Meanwhile, the University of Pécs, founded in 1367, became a renowned center of learning and scholarship, attracting students and scholars from far and wide.

Despite its cultural achievements, medieval Hungary was not immune to internal conflicts and external pressures. The rise of rival dynasties, such as the Angevins and the Habsburgs, and the ever-present threat of Ottoman expansion posed significant challenges to Hungary's sovereignty and stability. Nevertheless, the medieval era laid the groundwork for Hungary's subsequent development and left an indelible mark on its identity, heritage, and national consciousness.

Ottoman Rule and Habsburg Influence: Shaping Hungary's Destiny

The period of Ottoman rule and Habsburg influence stands as a pivotal chapter in Hungary's history, shaping its destiny in profound and lasting ways. Following the Battle of Mohács in 1526, where the Hungarian forces suffered a devastating defeat at the hands of the Ottoman Empire, Hungary fell under the sphere of Ottoman influence. The ensuing decades saw Hungary divided into three parts: the Ottoman-occupied territories in the south, the Habsburg-controlled regions in the west and north, and the semi-independent Principality of Transylvania in the east.

Ottoman rule brought significant changes to Hungary, both politically and culturally. The Ottomans established a system of governance based on the millet system, which granted certain religious and cultural freedoms to non-Muslim communities, including the Christian population in Hungary. However, Hungarian society was deeply affected by the imposition of Islamic law, the introduction of new administrative structures, and the levying of taxes and tribute.

The Habsburgs, ruling from Vienna, sought to counter Ottoman influence in Hungary and assert their own authority over the region. In 1541, Ferdinand I was crowned King of Hungary by the Hungarian nobility, establishing the Habsburgs as rulers of the western and northern territories. The

Habsburgs pursued a policy of centralization and Catholicization, seeking to integrate Hungary more closely into the Habsburg monarchy and promote Catholicism as the state religion.

The struggle for control over Hungary intensified in the 17th century, as the Ottoman Empire and the Habsburg monarchy engaged in a series of wars and conflicts known as the Long Turkish War. The Habsburgs, with the support of their allies, including the Holy Roman Empire and the Polish-Lithuanian Commonwealth, gradually pushed back the Ottoman forces and regained control over much of Hungary.

The Treaty of Karlowitz in 1699 marked the end of Ottoman rule in Hungary and the beginning of Habsburg hegemony over the entire kingdom. Hungary became an integral part of the Habsburg monarchy, with the Hungarian nobility pledging allegiance to the Habsburg emperor and the Hungarian Diet serving as a legislative body within the framework of the Habsburg administration.

The Habsburg era brought both benefits and challenges to Hungary. On one hand, Hungary experienced a period of economic and cultural growth, as the Habsburgs invested in infrastructure, industry, and education. Budapest, which became the capital of Hungary in 1873, underwent a transformation into a modern metropolis, with the construction of grand boulevards, palaces, and public buildings.

On the other hand, Hungary's relationship with the Habsburg monarchy was marked by tensions and conflicts, particularly over issues of national identity, autonomy, and representation. The Hungarian nobility, led by figures such as Ferenc Deák and Lajos Kossuth, advocated for greater political rights and autonomy for Hungary within the Habsburg Empire, leading to the adoption of the Ausgleich, or Compromise, of 1867, which established the dual monarchy of Austria-Hungary.

The legacy of Ottoman rule and Habsburg influence continues to shape Hungary's identity and politics to this day. The scars of centuries of foreign domination and internal strife are evident in Hungary's complex relationship with its neighbors, its struggles with nationalism and identity, and its ongoing quest for sovereignty and self-determination. Yet, the resilience and spirit of the Hungarian people endure, a testament to their enduring commitment to freedom, justice, and national unity.

Revolution and Independence: The Struggle for Sovereignty

The chapter on Revolution and Independence illuminates a critical period in Hungary's history, where the quest for sovereignty and self-determination reached a crescendo. Throughout the 19th century, Hungary grappled with the forces of nationalism, liberalism, and social upheaval, as it sought to break free from the shackles of foreign domination and assert its identity as a nation-state.

The revolution of 1848, often referred to as the Hungarian Revolution or the Springtime of Nations, stands as a defining moment in Hungary's struggle for independence. Fueled by a wave of nationalist fervor and inspired by liberal ideals spreading across Europe, Hungarians rose up against the oppressive rule of the Habsburg monarchy. Led by figures such as Lajos Kossuth, Lajos Batthyány, and Sándor Petőfi, the revolutionaries demanded political reform, civil liberties, and Hungarian autonomy within the framework of the Habsburg Empire.

The revolution saw the adoption of the April Laws, a series of progressive reforms that granted greater political rights and freedoms to the Hungarian people. These laws established the Diet of Hungary as a legislative body, abolished serfdom, and instituted equality before the law. However, the revolution also faced staunch opposition from the Habsburg monarchy and its allies, including Russian and Austrian forces, who sought to crush the uprising and preserve their hegemony over Hungary.

The revolution ultimately ended in defeat for the Hungarians, as the combined forces of the Habsburgs and their allies quashed the uprising and reimposed imperial authority. The Hungarian leaders, including Kossuth and Batthyány, were forced into exile, and the April Laws were repealed. Yet, the spirit of resistance and defiance lived on, as Hungarians continued to agitate for reform and independence in the decades that followed.

The Compromise of 1867, also known as the Ausgleich, represented a significant turning point in Hungary's quest for sovereignty. Negotiated between the Hungarian nobility and the Habsburg emperor Franz Joseph I, the Ausgleich established the dual monarchy of Austria-Hungary, granting Hungary greater autonomy and self-governance within the Habsburg Empire. Hungary gained its own parliament, government, and administrative institutions, while remaining part of a common monarchy with Austria.

The Ausgleich ushered in a period of relative stability and prosperity for Hungary, as the country experienced economic growth, industrialization, and cultural revival. Budapest emerged as a vibrant center of commerce, culture, and innovation, attracting artists, intellectuals, and entrepreneurs from across Europe. Yet, tensions simmered beneath the surface, as Hungary grappled with issues of national identity, ethnic diversity, and social inequality.

The legacy of the revolution and the struggle for independence continues to shape Hungary's politics, society, and national consciousness to this day. The memory of the revolutionaries, who fought valiantly for freedom and democracy, remains alive in the hearts of Hungarians, inspiring future generations to uphold the values of liberty, justice, and sovereignty.

The World Wars and Hungary's Turbulent 20th Century

In the tumultuous landscape of the 20th century, Hungary found itself embroiled in the upheavals of two world wars, grappling with the repercussions of political turmoil, foreign occupation, and ideological conflict. The First World War, which erupted in 1914, thrust Hungary into the heart of a global conflagration, as the Austro-Hungarian Empire mobilized its forces to defend its interests in Europe. Hungary's participation in the war exacted a heavy toll on its society and economy, as thousands of Hungarian soldiers perished on the battlefields of the Eastern and Western fronts.

The aftermath of World War I brought seismic changes to Hungary's political landscape, as the disintegration of the Austro-Hungarian Empire and the Treaty of Trianon in 1920 redrawn Hungary's borders and drastically reduced its territory. Hungary lost two-thirds of its pre-war territory and over half of its population, including large Hungarian-speaking communities in neighboring countries. The treaty left Hungary reeling from the loss of its historic lands, fueling resentment and nationalist sentiments that would reverberate for decades to come.

The interwar period saw Hungary grapple with political instability, economic hardship, and social upheaval. The collapse of the Austro-Hungarian Empire gave rise to a fledgling Hungarian republic, which struggled to assert its authority amidst competing factions and ideological divisions. The rise of authoritarian and nationalist movements, such as the Arrow Cross Party and the Hungarian National Socialist Party, reflected growing discontent with the post-war order and a desire to restore Hungary's lost greatness.

The Great Depression of the 1930s further exacerbated Hungary's woes, plunging the country into economic turmoil and social unrest. Unemployment soared, living standards plummeted, and political extremism flourished, as Hungarians sought scapegoats for their plight. The government of Prime Minister Gyula Gömbös, which came to power in 1932, pursued a policy of authoritarianism and corporatism, seeking to restore order and stability through centralized control and state intervention.

The outbreak of World War II in 1939 once again thrust Hungary into the maelstrom of global conflict, as the country aligned itself with Nazi Germany in pursuit of territorial expansion and national revival. Hungary's participation in the war saw its forces engaged in fierce battles on the Eastern and Balkan fronts, while at home, the Hungarian government collaborated with the Nazis in the persecution and deportation of Jews and other minorities. The Holocaust claimed the lives of over half a million Hungarian Jews, a tragic chapter in Hungary's history that continues to haunt the nation to this day.

The end of World War II brought a new era of hardship and uncertainty for Hungary, as the country fell under Soviet occupation and communist rule. The Hungarian Communist Party, led by Mátyás Rákosi, established a totalitarian regime that suppressed dissent, curtailed civil liberties, and imposed collectivization and state control over the economy. Hungary became a satellite state of the Soviet Union, subject to Moscow's dictates and ideological orthodoxy.

The post-war period also witnessed a series of uprisings and protests against communist rule, culminating in the Hungarian Revolution of 1956. Sparked by student demonstrations and worker strikes in Budapest, the revolution quickly escalated into a nationwide uprising against Soviet domination and communist oppression. Hungarian insurgents, led by figures such as Imre Nagy and János Kádár, demanded political reform, democratic elections, and Hungarian independence from Soviet influence.

The revolution, however, was brutally crushed by Soviet tanks and troops, as Moscow moved decisively to quash the uprising and restore communist control. Thousands of Hungarians were killed, wounded, or imprisoned in the aftermath of the revolution, while hundreds of thousands fled the country in fear of reprisals. The suppression of the revolution dealt a severe blow to Hungary's aspirations for freedom and democracy, ushering in a period of renewed repression and political stagnation under Soviet-backed rule.

The collapse of the Soviet Union in 1991 brought an end to communist rule in Hungary and the dawn of a new era of freedom and democracy. Hungary embarked on a path of political and economic reform, embracing liberal democracy, market capitalism, and European integration. The country joined NATO in 1999 and the European Union in 2004, signaling its return to the community of Western democracies and its commitment to shared values of liberty, prosperity, and peace.

Yet, the legacy of Hungary's turbulent 20th century continues to shape its identity, politics, and society in profound ways. The scars of war, occupation, and totalitarianism remain etched in the collective memory of Hungarians, serving as a reminder of the fragility of freedom and the resilience of the human spirit. As Hungary navigates the challenges and opportunities of the 21st century, its tumultuous past serves as a beacon of hope and a call to vigilance, inspiring future generations to cherish and defend the hard-won gains of liberty and democracy.

Post-Communist Era: Transition and Transformation

The post-communist era in Hungary heralded a period of profound transition and transformation, as the country emerged from decades of communist rule and embarked on a journey of political, economic, and social reform. With the collapse of the Soviet Union in 1991, Hungary, like other former Eastern Bloc nations, found itself at a crossroads, grappling with the challenges of building a new democratic order and market economy while navigating the legacies of its communist past.

The transition from communism to democracy was not without its challenges. Hungary's communist regime, led by the Hungarian Socialist Workers' Party, had stifled political dissent, suppressed civil liberties, and maintained tight control over the economy and media. The dismantling of the communist system and the establishment of democratic institutions required a delicate balance of political negotiation, societal reconciliation, and institutional reform.

In the early years of the post-communist era, Hungary implemented a series of political and economic reforms aimed at democratization and marketization. The first free elections in 1990 saw the Hungarian Democratic Forum emerge as the dominant political force, ushering in a period of coalition governments and political pluralism.

Hungary also embarked on a program of economic liberalization, privatization, and deregulation, aimed at transitioning from a centrally planned economy to a market-based system.

The transition to a market economy, however, brought with it challenges of its own. The shock therapy approach to economic reform, characterized by rapid privatization and liberalization, led to widespread unemployment, social dislocation, and economic hardship for many Hungarians. The dismantling of state-owned industries and the withdrawal of government subsidies exposed vulnerabilities in the Hungarian economy and exacerbated inequalities between urban and rural areas.

Despite the challenges, Hungary made significant strides in its transition to democracy and market economy. The country held multiple free and fair elections, established a multiparty system, and adopted a new constitution in 2011, which enshrined democratic principles, human rights, and the rule of law. Hungary also embarked on a path of European integration, joining the European Union in 2004 and adopting the euro as its currency in 2008.

The post-communist era also saw Hungary grapple with issues of societal transformation and identity. The transition from communism to capitalism brought about profound changes in Hungarian society, as traditional values clashed with modernity, and new social inequalities emerged. The rise of consumerism, globalization, and cultural pluralism challenged traditional norms and identities, sparking debates over Hungary's place in Europe and the world.

At the same time, Hungary experienced a resurgence of nationalist and populist sentiment, fueled by economic uncertainty, social dislocation, and disillusionment with mainstream politics. The rise of the far-right Jobbik party and the populist Fidesz party reflected growing discontent with the political establishment and a desire for strong leadership and national sovereignty. The government of Prime Minister Viktor Orbán, in particular, pursued a nationalist agenda that emphasized Hungarian identity, sovereignty, and cultural conservatism.

The post-communist era in Hungary remains a complex and contested chapter in the country's history, marked by both progress and setbacks, achievements and challenges. As Hungary navigates the uncertainties of the 21st century, its experiences in the post-communist era serve as a reminder of the enduring quest for democracy, freedom, and prosperity, and the need to confront the legacies of the past while forging a path towards a more inclusive and resilient future.

Budapest: Jewel of the Danube

Nestled along the banks of the majestic Danube River, Budapest stands as a true gem of Central Europe, captivating visitors with its timeless beauty, rich history, and vibrant culture. As the capital city of Hungary, Budapest serves as the beating heart of the nation, a dynamic metropolis that seamlessly blends old-world charm with modern sophistication.

Budapest's history dates back over a millennium, with traces of human settlement dating back to Roman times. Originally two separate cities—Buda and Pest—Budapest was united in 1873 to form a single, unified capital. Today, the city's skyline is dominated by iconic landmarks that reflect its storied past and architectural splendor.

One of Budapest's most recognizable landmarks is the Buda Castle, perched high atop Castle Hill overlooking the Danube. Originally built in the 13th century, the castle has been reconstructed and expanded over the centuries, serving as the residence of Hungarian kings and the seat of power for successive rulers. Today, the Buda Castle complex houses museums, galleries, and government offices, offering visitors a glimpse into Hungary's royal past.

Across the river lies Pest, the bustling commercial and cultural hub of Budapest. The city's iconic Parliament Building, with its neo-Gothic architecture and towering dome, is a testament to Hungary's democratic traditions and national pride.

Nearby, the grandeur of Andrássy Avenue unfolds, lined with elegant boulevards, stately mansions, and upscale boutiques, evoking the elegance of 19th-century Budapest.

But perhaps the most famous feature of Budapest's skyline is the Chain Bridge, an architectural marvel that spans the Danube and connects Buda and Pest. Built in 1849, the Chain Bridge was the first permanent bridge to link the two halves of the city, symbolizing unity and progress. Today, the bridge is not only a vital transportation artery but also a beloved landmark that offers breathtaking views of the cityscape.

Budapest's cultural scene is as vibrant as it is diverse, with a wealth of museums, theaters, and concert halls that cater to all tastes and interests. The Hungarian State Opera House, with its opulent interiors and world-class performances, is a must-visit for opera aficionados and architecture enthusiasts alike. Meanwhile, the Hungarian National Museum showcases the country's rich heritage and archaeological treasures, spanning from prehistory to the present day.

For those seeking relaxation and rejuvenation, Budapest's thermal baths offer a blissful retreat from the hustle and bustle of city life. The city is renowned for its numerous thermal springs, which have been revered for their healing properties since Roman times. Whether soaking in the mineral-rich waters of the Széchenyi Baths or indulging in a traditional Hungarian massage at the Gellért Baths, visitors can unwind and recharge in style.

Budapest's culinary scene is equally enticing, with a diverse array of restaurants, cafés, and markets that showcase the best of Hungarian cuisine. From hearty goulash and savory lángos to delicate pastries and fine wines, Budapest offers a gastronomic journey that delights the senses and satisfies the soul. The Central Market Hall, with its bustling stalls and aromatic flavors, is a food lover's paradise, offering a taste of Hungary's culinary heritage under one roof.

As day turns to night, Budapest comes alive with a vibrant nightlife that caters to every taste and mood. The city's ruin bars, housed in abandoned buildings and courtyards, offer a unique and eclectic atmosphere, where locals and visitors alike gather to socialize, sip cocktails, and dance the night away. Meanwhile, the banks of the Danube transform into a glittering spectacle, as the city's bridges and landmarks are illuminated against the backdrop of the night sky.

In every corner of Budapest, from its historic landmarks to its trendy neighborhoods, the spirit of Hungary's capital shines bright, inviting visitors to explore, discover, and savor all that this enchanting city has to offer. As Budapest continues to evolve and thrive in the 21st century, it remains a beacon of culture, creativity, and hospitality that captivates the hearts and imaginations of all who visit.

Exploring Historic Treasures: Must-See Sites in Budapest

In Budapest, every street corner holds a piece of history, a tale of bygone eras waiting to be discovered. As you wander through the city's labyrinthine streets, you'll encounter a wealth of historic treasures that reflect Budapest's rich and diverse heritage. One of the most iconic sites is the Buda Castle, perched majestically atop Castle Hill, offering panoramic views of the city below. Steeped in centuries of royal history, the castle complex houses the Hungarian National Gallery, the Budapest History Museum, and the Matthias Church, each offering insight into Hungary's storied past. Nearby, the Fisherman's Bastion stands as a fairy-tale fortress, with its whimsical turrets and panoramic terraces offering breathtaking views of the Danube and beyond.

Crossing the Danube, you'll find yourself in Pest, where the city's architectural splendors await. The Hungarian Parliament Building, with its neo-Gothic façade and towering dome, is a masterpiece of Hungarian craftsmanship and political symbolism. Nearby, St. Stephen's Basilica beckons with its grandeur and magnificence, housing the mummified hand of Hungary's patron saint, King Stephen. Meanwhile, the Great Synagogue, the largest synagogue in Europe, stands as a testament to Budapest's vibrant Jewish heritage, with its Moorish-inspired architecture and poignant Holocaust memorial.

As you delve deeper into Budapest's historic treasures, you'll encounter hidden gems tucked away in its winding streets and leafy squares. The Dohány Street Synagogue, with its exquisite Moorish Revival architecture and poignant Holocaust memorial, offers a somber reminder of Hungary's Jewish heritage and the atrocities of the past. Meanwhile, the House of Terror, housed in the former headquarters of the communist secret police, provides a chilling glimpse into Hungary's tumultuous 20th-century history, with exhibits dedicated to the victims of fascism and communism.

No exploration of Budapest's historic treasures would be complete without a visit to its thermal baths, which have been soothing weary souls for centuries. The Széchenyi Baths, housed in a grand neo-Baroque palace, offer a luxurious escape into thermal pools, saunas, and steam rooms, while the Gellért Baths, with their Art Nouveau splendor, provide a tranquil oasis amidst the hustle and bustle of city life.

As you navigate Budapest's historic sites, you'll encounter layers of history, culture, and tradition that span centuries and continents. From the grandeur of royal palaces to the somber reminders of wartime atrocities, Budapest's historic treasures offer a window into Hungary's complex and multifaceted past, inviting visitors to explore, discover, and reflect on the forces that have shaped this vibrant and resilient city.

Beyond Budapest: Exploring Hungary's Other Major Cities

Beyond the grandeur of Budapest lie several other major cities in Hungary, each with its own unique charm, history, and cultural significance. One such city is Debrecen, often referred to as the "Capital of the Great Plain." Debrecen boasts a rich heritage as a center of Hungarian Protestantism and played a pivotal role in the country's struggle for independence. Visitors can explore the city's historic landmarks, including the Great Reformed Church, which served as the site of Hungary's declaration of independence in 1849, and the Déri Museum, home to an impressive collection of Hungarian art and artifacts.

Another major city worth exploring is Szeged, located on the banks of the Tisza River in southern Hungary. Szeged is renowned for its stunning architecture, vibrant cultural scene, and thermal baths. The city's iconic Votive Church, with its intricate neo-Romanesque design and towering dome, is a testament to Szeged's resilience and renewal following a devastating flood in 1879. Visitors can also relax and unwind at the Szeged Thermal Bath, which offers a range of therapeutic treatments and relaxation facilities.

Further west, the city of Pécs beckons with its rich history and Mediterranean charm. Pécs is one of Hungary's oldest cities, with a history dating back over 2,000 years. Visitors can explore Pécs' well-preserved Roman ruins, including the Early Christian Necropolis, a UNESCO World Heritage site featuring ancient tombs and mausoleums. Pécs is also known for its vibrant arts scene, with numerous galleries, museums, and cultural events that showcase the city's creative spirit and multicultural heritage.

In the north of Hungary, the city of Győr offers a blend of medieval charm and modern amenities. Győr's historic old town, with its cobblestone streets and Baroque architecture, transports visitors back in time to Hungary's medieval past. The city's captivating sights include the Széchenyi Square, the Bishop's Castle, and the stunning Rába Quelle Thermal Spa, where visitors can relax in healing thermal waters and enjoy a range of wellness treatments.

Last but not least, the city of Székesfehérvár, located in central Hungary, boasts a rich history as the coronation and burial site of Hungarian kings and queens. Székesfehérvár's royal legacy is evident in its impressive medieval architecture, including the ruins of the medieval royal palace and the imposing Bory Castle, a whimsical fortress built by the eccentric architect Jenő Bory. Visitors can also explore the city's vibrant cultural scene, with theaters, galleries, and festivals that celebrate Hungary's artistic heritage.

In each of these major cities, visitors can discover a wealth of history, culture, and natural beauty that reflects the diverse and dynamic spirit of Hungary. From the medieval streets of Győr to the thermal baths of Szeged, Hungary's other major cities offer a captivating glimpse into the country's past, present, and future.

Pécs: A Journey Through History and Culture

Pécs, a city steeped in history and culture, beckons visitors to embark on a captivating journey through time. Located in the southern region of Hungary, Pécs boasts a heritage that spans over two millennia, making it one of the country's oldest and most storied cities. With its ancient ruins, medieval monuments, and vibrant arts scene, Pécs offers a wealth of experiences for travelers eager to explore its rich tapestry of heritage.

One of Pécs' most enduring legacies is its Roman past, dating back to the 2nd century AD when the city was known as Sopianae. Visitors can discover remnants of this ancient era at the Early Christian Necropolis, a UNESCO World Heritage site that features intricately carved tombs and mausoleums. The presence of these well-preserved Roman ruins serves as a poignant reminder of Pécs' role as a thriving urban center in the ancient world.

As the Roman Empire declined, Pécs fell under the rule of various medieval kingdoms and empires, including the Kingdom of Hungary and the Ottoman Empire. The city's medieval heritage is evident in its architectural landmarks, such as the Pécs Cathedral, a masterpiece of Romanesque and Gothic design, and the Pécs Synagogue, one of the largest synagogues in Europe. These historic sites offer visitors a glimpse into Pécs' medieval past and its role as a center of religious and cultural exchange.

Pécs reached new heights of prosperity and prestige during the Renaissance and Baroque periods, as evidenced by the city's elegant palaces, churches, and public squares. The Pécs Cathedral, with its ornate façade and towering spires, is a testament to the city's artistic and architectural achievements during this golden age. Meanwhile, the Zsolnay Cultural Quarter, named after the renowned Hungarian ceramics manufacturer, showcases Pécs' modern artistic prowess, with galleries, studios, and exhibitions that celebrate the city's creative spirit.

Today, Pécs is known for its vibrant arts scene, with numerous galleries, museums, and cultural events that showcase the city's diverse heritage and contemporary creativity. The Pécs Gallery, housed in a historic Baroque building, features a diverse collection of Hungarian and international art, while the Pécs Museum offers insights into the city's archaeological treasures and ethnographic traditions. Pécs' annual events, such as the Pécs International Jazz Festival and the Pécs National Theatre Festival, attract visitors from far and wide, highlighting the city's reputation as a cultural capital of Hungary.

In every corner of Pécs, from its ancient ruins to its modern cultural institutions, visitors can embark on a journey through history and culture that reveals the soul of this captivating city. With its rich heritage, vibrant arts scene, and warm hospitality, Pécs invites travelers to discover the timeless allure of Hungary's southern gem.

Debrecen: Gateway to the Great Hungarian Plain

Nestled in the heart of Hungary's Great Plain, Debrecen serves as the gateway to a vast expanse of fertile farmland, open skies, and boundless horizons. As the second-largest city in Hungary, Debrecen holds a special place in the country's cultural, economic, and educational landscape. With its rich history, vibrant cultural scene, and strategic location, Debrecen offers visitors a glimpse into the soul of Hungary's agricultural heartland.

Debrecen's history dates back over a millennium, with traces of human settlement found as far back as the Roman era. Over the centuries, the city evolved into a thriving center of trade, commerce, and religious life, earning it the nickname "Calvinist Rome" for its strong Protestant heritage. The Great Reformed Church, with its iconic twin towers and soaring dome, stands as a testament to Debrecen's religious significance and architectural prowess, serving as a focal point for the city's spiritual and cultural life.

Beyond its religious heritage, Debrecen is known for its role in Hungary's struggle for independence and national identity. In 1849, the city hosted the National Assembly of Hungary, where the country's declaration of independence was proclaimed, marking a pivotal moment in Hungary's quest for self-determination. Today, visitors can explore the historic sites associated with this period, including the Debrecen House of Parliament and the Déri Museum, which houses artifacts related to Hungary's revolutionary past.

Debrecen's strategic location at the crossroads of major trade routes has made it a vital hub of commerce, transportation, and education. The city is home to the University of Debrecen, one of Hungary's leading institutions of higher learning, attracting students from across the country and around the world. The university's sprawling campus, with its modern facilities and vibrant student life, contributes to Debrecen's dynamic and cosmopolitan atmosphere.

In addition to its cultural and educational institutions, Debrecen boasts a thriving arts scene, with numerous theaters, galleries, and cultural events that showcase the city's creative spirit. The Csokonai Theatre, named after the renowned Hungarian poet Mihály Csokonai Vitéz, hosts a variety of performances, from classical dramas to contemporary plays, while the MODEM Centre for Modern and Contemporary Arts showcases cutting-edge works by Hungarian and international artists.

As the gateway to the Great Hungarian Plain, Debrecen offers visitors the opportunity to explore the natural beauty and cultural heritage of Hungary's countryside. The Hortobágy National Park, located just outside the city, is a UNESCO World Heritage site and the largest protected area in Hungary, known for its vast grasslands, unique wildlife, and traditional shepherd culture. Visitors can explore the park on foot, by bicycle, or on horseback, experiencing the timeless allure of Hungary's rural landscape.

In every corner of Debrecen, from its historic landmarks to its modern amenities, visitors can discover a city that embodies the spirit of Hungary's Great Plain. With its rich history, vibrant culture, and warm hospitality, Debrecen invites travelers to experience the essence of Hungarian life in the heart of the countryside.

Szeged: Where Tradition Meets Innovation

In the sun-kissed region of southern Hungary lies Szeged, a city where tradition seamlessly intertwines with innovation to create a dynamic cultural tapestry. With its picturesque setting along the banks of the Tisza River and its rich history dating back over a millennium, Szeged captivates visitors with its charm, vitality, and distinctive blend of old-world charm and modern sophistication.

At the heart of Szeged lies its vibrant city center, where centuries-old buildings stand side by side with contemporary structures, reflecting the city's evolution over time. The Szeged Cathedral, with its majestic neo-Romanesque façade and towering spires, is a testament to the city's religious heritage and architectural prowess, drawing visitors from far and wide to admire its beauty and grandeur. Nearby, the Szeged Synagogue, one of the largest synagogues in Europe, stands as a poignant reminder of Szeged's rich Jewish heritage and cultural diversity.

As one of Hungary's leading educational and cultural centers, Szeged boasts a thriving arts scene that celebrates both tradition and innovation. The city is home to the University of Szeged, one of the country's oldest and most prestigious universities, renowned for its academic excellence and groundbreaking research. The university's vibrant campus, with its historic buildings and modern facilities, fosters a spirit of creativity and intellectual curiosity that permeates the city's cultural landscape.

Szeged's commitment to innovation is also evident in its thriving culinary scene, where traditional Hungarian cuisine meets contemporary gastronomy. The city's bustling markets, such as the Szeged Market Hall, offer a feast for the senses, with vendors selling fresh produce, artisanal cheeses, and aromatic spices. Meanwhile, Szeged's eclectic mix of restaurants and cafés serve up a diverse array of dishes, from hearty goulash and savory lángos to innovative fusion cuisine that reflects the city's cosmopolitan spirit.

In addition to its culinary delights, Szeged is known for its rich cultural heritage and vibrant arts scene. The city hosts numerous festivals and events throughout the year, showcasing a wide range of music, dance, theater, and visual arts. The Szeged Open-Air Festival, held annually in the city's Dóm Square, is one of Hungary's premier cultural events, attracting thousands of visitors with its world-class performances and lively atmosphere.

Beyond its cultural attractions, Szeged is also a haven for nature lovers, with its scenic parks, gardens, and riverfront promenades. The Szeged Botanical Garden, with its diverse collection of plants and flowers, offers a peaceful retreat from the hustle and bustle of city life, while the banks of the Tisza River provide ample opportunities for outdoor recreation, including boating, fishing, and picnicking.

In every corner of Szeged, from its historic landmarks to its modern amenities, visitors can experience a city that embodies the spirit of Hungarian hospitality, creativity, and innovation. With its rich cultural heritage, vibrant arts scene, and stunning natural beauty, Szeged invites travelers to embark on a journey of discovery and exploration, where tradition meets innovation in perfect harmony.

Cultural Identity: Hungarian Folklore and Traditions

Hungarian culture is deeply rooted in a rich tapestry of folklore and traditions that have been passed down through generations, shaping the country's unique identity and sense of belonging. From vibrant folk music and dance to colorful festivals and rituals, Hungarian folklore is a testament to the resilience, creativity, and spirit of its people.

One of the most iconic elements of Hungarian folklore is its traditional music, characterized by haunting melodies, intricate rhythms, and soul-stirring lyrics. The Hungarian folk music tradition dates back centuries, with influences from various ethnic groups and regions across the country. Instruments such as the violin, clarinet, and cimbalom feature prominently in Hungarian folk music, creating a distinctive sound that resonates with listeners around the world.

Accompanying the music is Hungarian folk dance, a lively and energetic art form that celebrates the joys, sorrows, and everyday experiences of Hungarian life. Each region of Hungary boasts its own unique style of folk dance, with colorful costumes, intricate footwork, and spirited choreography that reflects the cultural diversity and regional identities of the country. Folk dance festivals and performances are popular events throughout Hungary, drawing participants and spectators from far and wide.

Hungarian folklore is also rich in symbolism, rituals, and superstitions that are deeply ingrained in the fabric of everyday life. From traditional folk costumes adorned with intricate embroidery and decorative motifs to elaborate wedding ceremonies steeped in age-old customs and traditions, Hungarian culture is a living expression of its folklore and heritage.

Throughout the year, Hungary comes alive with a vibrant calendar of festivals and celebrations that honor its folklore and traditions. From the colorful revelry of the Busójárás festival in Mohács to the solemn processions of Easter in Hollókő, each festival offers a unique glimpse into Hungarian culture and identity. Food also plays a central role in Hungarian festivals, with traditional dishes such as lángos, goulash, and kürtőskalács (chimney cake) enjoyed by revelers of all ages.

Religion has also played a significant role in shaping Hungarian folklore and traditions. Many Hungarian festivals and rituals have roots in Christian holidays and customs, such as Christmas, Easter, and Saint Stephen's Day. Religious icons, symbols, and rituals are woven into the fabric of everyday life, reflecting Hungary's deep spiritual heritage and sense of community.

In recent years, there has been a renewed interest in Hungarian folklore and traditions, with efforts to preserve and promote these cultural treasures for future generations. Folklore groups, museums, and educational programs across Hungary are working to safeguard traditional music, dance, crafts, and rituals, ensuring that Hungarian culture continues to thrive and evolve in the modern world.

Overall, Hungarian folklore and traditions are an integral part of the country's cultural identity, serving as a source of inspiration, pride, and unity for its people. Through music, dance, festivals, and rituals, Hungarians celebrate their heritage, honor their ancestors, and forge connections that transcend time and borders.

Festivals and Celebrations: A Calendar of Hungarian Culture

Hungary's cultural calendar is brimming with a colorful array of festivals and celebrations that reflect the country's rich heritage, traditions, and spirit of community. From ancient rituals rooted in pagan folklore to modern events that celebrate Hungary's diverse cultural landscape, the country offers something for everyone throughout the year.

One of Hungary's most famous festivals is the Busójárás, held in the town of Mohács during the period leading up to Lent. This centuries-old tradition features elaborate costumes, masks, and folk music, as participants parade through the streets to drive away winter and welcome the arrival of spring. The Busójárás is a vibrant celebration of Hungarian folklore and community spirit, attracting visitors from far and wide to witness its colorful spectacle.

Another highlight of Hungary's cultural calendar is Easter, a time of religious observance and festive traditions. Hungarian Easter celebrations often include elaborate egg decorating, traditional dishes such as ham and Easter bread, and religious services commemorating the resurrection of Jesus Christ. In villages like Hollókő, Easter is celebrated with ancient rituals and processions that have been passed down through generations, offering a glimpse into Hungary's deep spiritual heritage.

Summer in Hungary brings a host of outdoor festivals and events that showcase the country's vibrant cultural scene. One of the most popular summer festivals is the Sziget Festival, held annually on Óbudai Island in Budapest. This weeklong extravaganza features live music, art installations, and performances by artists from around the world, drawing hundreds of thousands of music lovers to the banks of the Danube each year.

As autumn approaches, Hungary comes alive with harvest festivals and wine celebrations that honor the country's agricultural heritage. In the wine-growing regions of Tokaj, Eger, and Villány, grape harvest festivals are held to celebrate the bounty of the vineyards and the art of winemaking. These festivals feature wine tastings, traditional music and dance, and culinary delights that showcase Hungary's rich gastronomic traditions.

In December, Hungary transforms into a winter wonderland with festive Christmas markets and holiday celebrations that light up the streets and squares of cities and towns across the country. Budapest's Christmas markets, held in iconic locations such as Vörösmarty Square and St. Stephen's Basilica, offer a magical atmosphere with twinkling lights, seasonal decorations, and an array of handmade crafts and gifts. Visitors can sample traditional Hungarian delicacies like kürtőskalács (chimney cake), mulled wine, and roasted chestnuts as they soak in the holiday spirit.

Throughout the year, Hungary's festivals and celebrations provide opportunities for locals and visitors alike to come together, celebrate their heritage, and create lasting memories. From ancient traditions to modern cultural events, these festivals showcase the diversity, creativity, and resilience of Hungarian culture, ensuring that its traditions continue to thrive and evolve in the 21st century.

The Puszta: Exploring Hungary's Great Plain and Wildlife

The Puszta, or the Great Hungarian Plain, stretches across the eastern part of Hungary, encompassing vast expanses of flat grassland, meandering rivers, and scattered farms and villages. Covering approximately half of Hungary's territory, the Puszta is one of the largest and most distinctive natural regions in Europe, known for its unique landscapes, rich biodiversity, and traditional way of life.

One of the defining features of the Puszta is its expansive grasslands, which stretch as far as the eye can see, interrupted only by occasional patches of forest and clusters of trees. This open landscape is ideal habitat for a diverse range of wildlife, including numerous species of birds, mammals, and reptiles. The Puszta is home to iconic species such as the great bustard, Europe's heaviest flying bird, as well as the imperial eagle, the saker falcon, and the European souslik, a type of ground squirrel.

The Puszta's wetlands and marshes provide important habitat for migratory birds, making it a haven for birdwatchers and nature enthusiasts. The Hortobágy National Park, located in the heart of the Puszta, is a UNESCO World Heritage site and one of Europe's largest natural reserves, protecting the region's unique ecosystems and wildlife. Visitors to the park can explore its network of walking trails, observation towers, and bird hides, offering opportunities to observe rare and endangered species in their natural habitat.

In addition to its wildlife, the Puszta is also home to traditional Hungarian horsemen known as csikós, who have been herding horses on the plains for centuries. The csikós are skilled equestrians who demonstrate their horsemanship and herding techniques during performances known as puszta five. These displays, which feature daring feats of riding and lassoing, showcase the close bond between the csikós and their horses and offer a glimpse into Hungary's equestrian heritage.

The Puszta's traditional way of life is also reflected in its architecture, cuisine, and cultural traditions. Traditional farmsteads, known as tanyas, dot the landscape, with their distinctive thatched roofs and whitewashed walls. The cuisine of the Puszta is hearty and rustic, featuring dishes such as gulyás (goulash), pörkölt (stew), and töltött káposzta (stuffed cabbage), made from locally sourced ingredients such as beef, pork, and vegetables.

Throughout the year, the Puszta comes alive with festivals and celebrations that celebrate its natural beauty and cultural heritage. The Hortobágy Equestrian Days, held annually in August, feature horse shows, folk music and dance performances, and traditional crafts demonstrations, attracting visitors from across Hungary and beyond. Other events, such as the Hortobágy Shepherd's Festival and the Crane Festival, offer opportunities to experience the rich traditions and folklore of the Puszta firsthand.

In every corner of the Puszta, from its vast grasslands to its traditional villages, visitors can discover a landscape that is both timeless and dynamic, where nature and culture converge in a harmonious tapestry of life. Whether exploring its wildlife, experiencing its cultural traditions, or simply taking in its sweeping vistas, the Puszta offers a unique and unforgettable journey through Hungary's Great Plain.

Danube Delta: Nature's Splendor Along Hungary's Waterways

The Danube Delta, a UNESCO World Heritage site, is a sprawling wetland paradise located in southeastern Europe, where the mighty Danube River meets the Black Sea. While the majority of the delta lies within Romania, a portion of this breathtaking natural wonder extends into Hungary, offering visitors a chance to experience its unparalleled beauty and biodiversity. Covering over 1,600 square miles, the Danube Delta is Europe's second-largest river delta and home to an astonishing array of plant and animal life.

The delta's labyrinthine network of channels, lakes, and marshes creates a dynamic and ever-changing landscape, shaped by the ebb and flow of the Danube River and the tides of the Black Sea. These waterways are teeming with life, supporting over 300 species of birds, including pelicans, herons, egrets, and cormorants, making it one of the most important birdwatching destinations in Europe. The delta is also home to numerous species of fish, amphibians, and mammals, including the elusive European otter and the endangered Danube Delta horse.

One of the most iconic features of the Danube Delta is its vast expanses of reed beds, which provide habitat for a diverse range of bird species and serve as a vital nesting and breeding ground. Visitors to the delta can explore these reed beds by boat, kayak, or canoe, immersing themselves in the sights and sounds of this unique ecosystem. Along the way, they may encounter rare and elusive species such as the Dalmatian pelican, the white-tailed eagle, and the pygmy cormorant.

The delta's wetlands are also home to a rich diversity of plant life, including water lilies, bulrushes, and willow trees, which thrive in the delta's nutrient-rich soils and temperate climate. In the spring and summer months, the delta bursts into bloom with colorful wildflowers, creating a vibrant tapestry of colors and fragrances that captivates the senses.

In addition to its natural beauty, the Danube Delta is also a haven for outdoor enthusiasts, offering opportunities for fishing, boating, birdwatching, and wildlife photography. Visitors can explore the delta's waterways on guided boat tours, discovering hidden channels, secluded lagoons, and pristine beaches that are inaccessible by land. Fishing enthusiasts can try their luck at catching a variety of freshwater fish, including carp, pike, and catfish, while birdwatchers can spot rare and migratory species from observation towers and bird hides scattered throughout the delta.

The Danube Delta is not only a haven for wildlife but also a vital ecosystem that provides numerous ecological benefits, including flood control, water filtration, and carbon sequestration. Recognizing its importance, efforts are underway to protect and preserve the delta's natural habitats and biodiversity for future generations to enjoy. Through sustainable tourism practices and conservation initiatives, the Danube Delta remains a shining example of nature's splendor along Hungary's waterways, inviting visitors to experience its beauty and wonder firsthand.

Hungarian Vineyards and Wines: A Toast to Tradition

In the rolling hills and fertile valleys of Hungary, vineyards have been cultivated for centuries, yielding wines that are celebrated for their quality, diversity, and distinctive character. Hungarian winemaking has a long and storied history, dating back to the Roman era, when vines were first introduced to the region. Over the centuries, Hungary has become renowned for its unique grape varieties, terroir-driven wines, and rich winemaking traditions that continue to thrive to this day.

One of Hungary's most famous wine regions is Tokaj, located in the northeast part of the country. Tokaj has been producing wine for over a thousand years and is best known for its sweet, botrytized wines made from the furmint and hárslevelű grape varieties. These wines, known as Tokaji Aszú, are made using a traditional method known as "noble rot," where grapes are left to shrivel on the vine, concentrating their sugars and flavors. Tokaji Aszú has been prized by royalty and connoisseurs alike for its complex aromas, luscious sweetness, and exceptional aging potential.

In addition to Tokaj, Hungary is home to several other prominent wine regions, each with its own unique terroir and grape varieties. The Eger region, located in the northeast, is famous for its bold and spicy red wines, particularly Egri Bikavér, or "Bull's Blood," a blend of indigenous and international grape varieties. Meanwhile, the Villány region, located in the south, is known for its full-bodied red wines made from the cabernet sauvignon, cabernet franc, and merlot grapes, which thrive in the region's warm climate and limestone-rich soils. Hungarian winemakers are also experimenting with international grape varieties, such as chardonnay, sauvignon blanc, and pinot noir, with great success. These wines, often labeled as "fekete" or "white" wines, offer a modern twist on traditional Hungarian winemaking, appealing to a new generation of wine enthusiasts both at home and abroad.

In recent years, there has been a renewed interest in Hungarian wine, both domestically and internationally, with Hungarian wines earning accolades and recognition on the global stage. The country's diverse wine regions, coupled with its long winemaking tradition and innovative spirit, have positioned Hungary as an exciting and dynamic wine-producing nation.

Hungarian wines are also celebrated for their versatility and food-friendliness, pairing well with a wide range of cuisines and dishes. Whether enjoyed on their own or paired with traditional Hungarian fare such as goulash, paprikash, or lángos, Hungarian wines offer a taste of tradition and terroir that is sure to delight the senses and stimulate the palate.

In every glass of Hungarian wine, there is a story to be told – of centuries-old traditions, of innovative winemakers, and of the unique landscapes and climates that shape each bottle. As Hungary's winemaking renaissance continues to unfold, wine lovers around the world are raising their glasses to toast to the country's rich winemaking heritage and promising future.

Architectural Marvels: From Castles to Thermal Baths

Hungary's architectural landscape is a testament to its rich and diverse history, spanning centuries of influence from various cultures and civilizations. From medieval castles perched on rugged hilltops to opulent thermal baths adorned with intricate mosaics, Hungary boasts an array of architectural marvels that reflect its cultural heritage, ingenuity, and craftsmanship.

One of Hungary's most iconic architectural landmarks is Buda Castle, located in the heart of Budapest atop Castle Hill. Originally built in the 13th century, Buda Castle has undergone numerous renovations and expansions over the centuries, resulting in a magnificent complex of palaces, courtyards, and gardens that overlook the Danube River. The castle's Gothic, Renaissance, and Baroque elements are a testament to Hungary's royal past and its enduring legacy as a seat of power and prestige.

Another jewel of Hungarian architecture is Matthias Church, located adjacent to Buda Castle in Budapest's Castle District. This stunning Gothic-style church dates back to the 14th century and boasts a richly decorated interior adorned with frescoes, stained glass windows, and ornate altars. Matthias Church has played a central role in Hungary's religious and cultural life for centuries, hosting coronations, weddings, and other important ceremonies throughout its storied history.

In addition to its medieval castles and churches, Hungary is renowned for its thermal baths, which have been enjoyed for their therapeutic properties since Roman times. Budapest alone is home to over 100 thermal springs, making it one of the world's premier spa destinations. The Széchenyi Thermal Bath, located in City Park, is one of Budapest's most popular thermal baths, featuring a stunning Neo-Baroque architectural style and a range of indoor and outdoor pools, saunas, and steam rooms.

Another architectural gem in Budapest is the Hungarian Parliament Building, situated on the banks of the Danube River. This imposing Gothic Revival-style building is the largest parliament building in Europe and serves as a symbol of Hungary's national identity and democratic heritage. With its intricate façade, towering spires, and grand interiors, the Hungarian Parliament Building is a masterpiece of architecture and a must-see landmark for visitors to Budapest.

Outside of Budapest, Hungary is dotted with charming towns and villages that boast their own architectural treasures. The town of Eger, for example, is known for its beautifully preserved Baroque buildings, including the Eger Castle and the Eger Cathedral. Meanwhile, the village of Hollókő, a UNESCO World Heritage site, is renowned for its traditional Hungarian architecture, with whitewashed houses, thatched roofs, and cobblestone streets that harken back to a bygone era.

From medieval castles to ornate churches, from opulent palaces to soothing thermal baths, Hungary's architectural marvels offer a glimpse into the country's rich history, culture, and craftsmanship. Whether exploring the grandeur of Budapest's landmarks or discovering the hidden gems of Hungary's countryside, visitors are sure to be enchanted by the beauty and diversity of Hungary's architectural heritage.

The Legacy of the Austro-Hungarian Empire: Art, Architecture, and Influence

The Austro-Hungarian Empire, which existed from 1867 to 1918, left a lasting legacy on the cultural landscape of Central Europe, shaping art, architecture, and society in profound ways. This dual monarchy, formed through the Austro-Hungarian Compromise, brought together the Austrian Empire and the Kingdom of Hungary under a shared monarchy, creating a powerful and influential union that spanned diverse ethnic and linguistic groups.

One of the most significant contributions of the Austro-Hungarian Empire was its patronage of the arts, which flourished during this period. Vienna, the imperial capital of the empire, became a vibrant cultural center, attracting artists, writers, musicians, and intellectuals from across Europe. The Vienna Secession movement, founded in 1897, sought to break away from traditional artistic conventions and embrace modernism in all its forms. Artists such as Gustav Klimt, Egon Schiele, and Otto Wagner were key figures in the Vienna Secession, producing innovative works that challenged prevailing artistic norms and paved the way for the development of modern art. In addition to Vienna, Budapest, the capital of Hungary, also experienced a cultural renaissance during the Austro-Hungarian Empire. The city's architecture, in particular, was greatly influenced by the eclectic styles of the period, blending elements of Gothic, Renaissance, Baroque, and Art Nouveau architecture to create a distinctive urban landscape.

Iconic landmarks such as the Hungarian Parliament Building, the Széchenyi Chain Bridge, and the Hungarian State Opera House are testament to the empire's architectural legacy in Budapest.

The Austro-Hungarian Empire also left its mark on the cultural and intellectual life of its diverse population. The empire's policy of dualism, which granted significant autonomy to Hungary while maintaining close ties with Austria, fostered a sense of national identity and pride among Hungarians. Hungarian literature, music, and theater flourished during this period, with artists such as Ferenc Liszt, Béla Bartók, and Zoltán Kodály making significant contributions to the country's cultural heritage. At the same time, the empire's multinational character created a rich tapestry of ethnic diversity, with Germans, Czechs, Slovaks, Poles, Ukrainians, Romanians, and other ethnic groups coexisting within its borders. While this diversity was a source of strength and vitality for the empire, it also contributed to tensions and conflicts that ultimately led to its dissolution following World War I.

Despite its eventual demise, the Austro-Hungarian Empire's legacy continues to be felt in the cultural, political, and social fabric of Central Europe. Its influence can be seen in the architectural landmarks that dot the region, the artistic movements that emerged during its heyday, and the enduring cultural traditions that have been passed down through generations. As a pivotal chapter in the history of Europe, the Austro-Hungarian Empire remains a source of fascination and inspiration for scholars, artists, and historians alike.

Music and Dance: The Heartbeat of Hungarian Culture

Music and dance lie at the very core of Hungarian culture, pulsating through the nation's veins with a rhythm that is both timeless and exhilarating. Rooted in centuries of tradition and shaped by a diverse array of influences, Hungarian music and dance reflect the country's rich tapestry of history, folklore, and identity.

At the heart of Hungarian music is the folk tradition, which encompasses a wide variety of styles and genres that have been passed down through generations. Traditional Hungarian folk music is characterized by its vibrant melodies, intricate rhythms, and emotive lyrics, which often tell stories of love, loss, and everyday life in the countryside. Instruments such as the violin, cimbalom, flute, and clarinet are commonly used in folk music ensembles, creating a rich and dynamic sound that is uniquely Hungarian.

One of the most iconic forms of Hungarian folk music is the csárdás, a lively dance that originated in the rural regions of Hungary and Transylvania. The csárdás is characterized by its fast-paced tempo, syncopated rhythms, and intricate footwork, which often involves rapid turns, leaps, and kicks. Accompanied by traditional folk music, the csárdás is a celebratory dance that is performed at weddings, festivals, and other social gatherings, serving as a joyful expression of Hungarian identity and community spirit.

In addition to folk music and dance, Hungary has a rich classical music tradition that has produced some of the world's most renowned composers and performers. One of the most famous Hungarian composers is Franz Liszt, whose virtuosic piano compositions and orchestral works have left an indelible mark on the world of classical music. Other notable Hungarian composers include Béla Bartók, Zoltán Kodály, and Franz Lehár, whose compositions draw inspiration from Hungarian folk music and cultural traditions.

Hungarian classical music is celebrated for its innovative harmonies, expressive melodies, and deep emotional resonance, which have captivated audiences around the world. The Budapest Festival Orchestra, founded by conductor Iván Fischer, is one of Hungary's premier orchestras, renowned for its dynamic performances and commitment to excellence in classical music.

In addition to folk and classical music, Hungary has also made significant contributions to the world of opera, ballet, and contemporary music. The Hungarian State Opera House in Budapest is one of Europe's most prestigious opera houses, hosting performances of both classic and modern operas by Hungarian and international artists. Meanwhile, the Hungarian National Ballet is celebrated for its innovative choreography and dynamic performances, showcasing the country's rich tradition of dance and movement.

From the lively rhythms of the csárdás to the soaring melodies of classical symphonies, Hungarian music and dance embody the spirit and soul of the nation, uniting people across generations and borders in a celebration of culture, creativity, and community. As Hungary continues to evolve and embrace new artistic expressions, its musical heritage remains a vibrant and enduring testament to the power of creativity and the human spirit.

Hungarian Literature: From Epic Poetry to Contemporary Prose

Hungarian literature boasts a rich and storied tradition that spans centuries, encompassing a diverse range of genres, styles, and themes. From epic poetry to contemporary prose, Hungarian writers have made significant contributions to the world of literature, exploring the human experience with depth, insight, and imagination.

One of the earliest works of Hungarian literature is the "Chronicle of the Hungarians," written by the chronicler Simon Kézai in the 13th century. This epic chronicle traces the history of the Hungarian people from their mythical origins to the reign of King Béla III, offering valuable insights into Hungary's medieval past and cultural identity.

In the 19th century, Hungarian literature experienced a golden age known as the "Romantic Period," characterized by a flowering of literary creativity and national consciousness. Writers such as Sándor Petőfi, János Arany, and Ferenc Kölcsey played pivotal roles in shaping the Hungarian literary landscape, producing works that celebrated the nation's history, folklore, and language.

One of the most famous poems of this period is Petőfi's "National Song," which became a rallying cry for Hungarian nationalism during the Revolution of 1848. Arany's epic poem "Toldi" is another classic of Hungarian literature, drawing inspiration from the country's medieval legends and heroic past.

In the early 20th century, Hungarian literature underwent a period of experimentation and innovation, with writers such as Endre Ady, Dezső Kosztolányi, and Mihály Babits exploring new literary forms and themes. Ady, known as the "poet of the nation," was a leading figure of Hungarian modernism, whose works challenged conventional poetic norms and embraced themes of social justice and political activism.

The interwar period saw the rise of Hungarian avant-garde literature, with writers such as Lajos Kassák, Attila József, and Gyula Illyés pushing the boundaries of literary expression and experimentation. József, in particular, is celebrated for his innovative use of language and his exploration of existential themes in works such as "The Seventh Candle" and "The Iron-Blue Vault."

Following World War II and the Communist takeover of Hungary, literature became a battleground for political and ideological struggles, with writers facing censorship and persecution for their dissenting views. Despite these challenges, Hungarian literature continued to flourish, with writers such as György Konrád, Péter Esterházy, and Magda Szabó producing works of profound depth and insight that captured the complexities of life under totalitarianism.

In the post-communist era, Hungarian literature has continued to evolve and adapt to changing cultural and social landscapes, with writers exploring themes of identity, memory, and transition in the wake of political upheaval. Contemporary Hungarian authors such as László Krasznahorkai, Péter Nádas, and Olga Tokarczuk have gained international acclaim for their bold and innovative storytelling, cementing Hungary's reputation as a powerhouse of literary talent and creativity.

From epic poetry to contemporary prose, Hungarian literature reflects the soul and spirit of a nation, capturing the essence of its history, culture, and collective imagination. As Hungary continues to navigate the complexities of the modern world, its literary tradition remains a beacon of wisdom, inspiration, and artistic excellence for generations to come.

Religion in Hungary: Faith and Heritage

Religion in Hungary is a multifaceted tapestry that reflects the country's rich and diverse cultural heritage. Throughout its history, Hungary has been shaped by various religious traditions, including Christianity, Judaism, Islam, and indigenous belief systems. Today, the majority of Hungarians identify as Christians, with the largest denomination being Roman Catholicism.

Christianity has deep roots in Hungarian history, dating back to the arrival of missionaries in the 10th century. Saint Stephen, Hungary's first king, played a pivotal role in establishing Christianity as the state religion, and his legacy continues to be celebrated in Hungarian culture and folklore. The Roman Catholic Church has long been a dominant force in Hungarian religious life, with many churches, cathedrals, and monasteries serving as important centers of worship and pilgrimage.

In addition to Roman Catholicism, Hungary is also home to significant Protestant and Eastern Orthodox communities. The Reformation, which swept through Europe in the 16th century, had a profound impact on Hungarian society, leading to the emergence of Protestant denominations such as Lutheranism and Calvinism. Today, Protestantism remains a vibrant and influential force in Hungarian religious life, with churches and congregations spread across the country.

Hungary's Jewish community has a long and storied history, dating back over a thousand years. Jewish settlers first arrived in Hungary during the Middle Ages, and over time, the community grew and flourished, contributing to the country's cultural, economic, and intellectual life. However, the Holocaust during World War II decimated Hungary's Jewish population, and although the community has since rebounded, it remains relatively small compared to pre-war numbers.

Islam also has a presence in Hungary, particularly in the southern regions of the country, where Ottoman rule left a lasting imprint on the landscape and culture. Today, Hungary's Muslim community is composed primarily of ethnic minorities, including Turks, Bosniaks, and Roma, who practice their faith in mosques and cultural centers scattered throughout the country.

In addition to organized religion, Hungary also has a rich tradition of indigenous belief systems and folk practices. Pagan rituals and customs, rooted in ancient Hungarian mythology and folklore, continue to be celebrated in festivals, holidays, and traditional ceremonies, preserving the country's cultural heritage and spiritual connection to the land.

Religion in Hungary is not just a matter of faith but also a reflection of the country's complex history, identity, and sense of community. As Hungary continues to evolve and embrace the challenges of the modern world, its religious landscape remains a vibrant and integral part of its cultural fabric, shaping the beliefs, values, and traditions of its people for generations to come.

Education and Intellectual Heritage: Hungary's Scholarly Legacy

Education and intellectual heritage are deeply ingrained in Hungary's cultural fabric, shaping the nation's identity and fostering a legacy of scholarly excellence that spans centuries. From its early beginnings as a center of learning in medieval Europe to its modern-day reputation as a hub of innovation and academic achievement, Hungary has played a pivotal role in the advancement of knowledge and ideas.

One of Hungary's most illustrious educational institutions is the University of Pécs, founded in 1367, making it one of the oldest universities in Europe. Over the centuries, the University of Pécs has been a beacon of learning and scholarship, attracting students and scholars from around the world to study and collaborate in fields ranging from medicine and law to humanities and natural sciences.

In addition to the University of Pécs, Hungary is also home to several other prestigious universities and research institutions, including Eötvös Loránd University in Budapest, founded in 1635, and the Budapest University of Technology and Economics, founded in 1782. These institutions have played a central role in shaping Hungary's intellectual landscape, producing generations of scholars, scientists, and leaders who have made significant contributions to their respective fields.

Hungary's commitment to education and intellectual inquiry is reflected in its rich literary and cultural heritage. Hungarian literature, in particular, has a long and storied tradition, with writers such as Sándor Márai, Imre Kertész, and Magda Szabó gaining international acclaim for their insightful and thought-provoking works. Hungarian literature has also been deeply influenced by the country's turbulent history, with writers grappling with themes of identity, memory, and the human condition in the face of political and social upheaval.

Hungary's intellectual legacy extends beyond the realm of literature to encompass a wide range of disciplines, including philosophy, science, and the arts. Hungarian thinkers such as László Lovász, John von Neumann, and Albert Szent-Györgyi have made groundbreaking contributions to mathematics, physics, and medicine, earning international recognition for their pioneering research and discoveries.

In addition to its achievements in academia and the sciences, Hungary has also made significant strides in the arts and humanities, with artists, musicians, and intellectuals enriching the cultural landscape with their creativity and vision. The Hungarian Academy of Sciences, founded in 1825, has played a central role in fostering scholarly inquiry and promoting intellectual exchange, serving as a forum for debate and collaboration among Hungary's leading thinkers and scholars.

As Hungary continues to embrace the challenges of the 21st century, its commitment to education and intellectual inquiry remains steadfast, driving innovation, creativity, and progress across all fields of endeavor. With a proud legacy of scholarship and intellectual achievement, Hungary stands as a testament to the enduring power of knowledge and the human spirit.

The Hungarian Language: An Introduction and Overview

The Hungarian language, also known as Magyar, is a unique and fascinating member of the Finno-Ugric language family, which includes Finnish and Estonian. It is spoken by approximately 10 million people worldwide, primarily in Hungary and neighboring regions, as well as by Hungarian diaspora communities around the globe.

One of the most distinctive features of the Hungarian language is its agglutinative nature, meaning that words are formed by adding suffixes and prefixes to a root word. This allows for the creation of complex words with multiple meanings and nuances, making Hungarian a highly expressive and versatile language.

The Hungarian alphabet consists of 44 letters, including 14 vowels and 30 consonants. It is written using the Latin script, with additional characters such as á, é, í, ó, ö, ő, ú, ü, ű, and accents used to indicate vowel length and pronunciation.

Hungarian grammar is characterized by a system of noun cases and verb conjugations, which determine the role and function of words within a sentence. There are 18 noun cases in Hungarian, including the nominative, accusative, dative, and genitive, each of which indicates a different grammatical relationship.

Verbs in Hungarian are conjugated according to tense, mood, aspect, and person, with different suffixes added to the verb stem to indicate these variations.

Hungarian verbs also conjugate for definiteness and specificity, allowing speakers to convey subtle distinctions in meaning and intention.

Hungarian vocabulary has been influenced by various languages and cultures throughout its history, including Latin, German, Turkish, and Slavic languages. This linguistic diversity has enriched the Hungarian lexicon, resulting in a rich tapestry of words and expressions that reflect the country's cultural heritage and historical legacy.

Despite its linguistic complexity, Hungarian is known for its logical and consistent grammar, which follows strict rules and patterns. This makes it a challenging but rewarding language to learn, with a rich literary tradition that includes works by renowned authors such as Sándor Márai, Magda Szabó, and Imre Kertész.

In addition to its literary heritage, Hungarian is also celebrated for its vibrant oral traditions, including folk tales, poetry, and songs, which have been passed down through generations and continue to be cherished as an integral part of Hungarian culture and identity.

Overall, the Hungarian language is a testament to the ingenuity and creativity of the Hungarian people, reflecting their unique history, traditions, and worldview. As Hungary continues to evolve and embrace the opportunities of the modern world, the Hungarian language remains a powerful symbol of national pride and cultural heritage, uniting people across generations and borders in a shared celebration of language and identity.

Hungarian Etiquette and Social Customs: Navigating Cultural Norms

Understanding Hungarian etiquette and social customs is essential for anyone looking to navigate the cultural landscape of Hungary with grace and respect. Hungarians place a strong emphasis on politeness, hospitality, and social hierarchy, and observing these customs can help forge meaningful connections and foster positive interactions with locals.

One of the most important aspects of Hungarian etiquette is the concept of respect for elders and authority figures. In Hungarian culture, age and experience are highly valued, and it is customary to address older individuals with deference and defer to their opinions and advice. When meeting someone for the first time, it is customary to address them by their title and last name, followed by the honorific "Úr" (Mr.) or "Asszony" (Mrs./Ms.).

Hospitality is also a cornerstone of Hungarian social customs, with hosts going to great lengths to make guests feel welcome and comfortable in their homes. When invited to a Hungarian home, it is customary to bring a small gift, such as flowers, chocolates, or a bottle of wine, as a token of appreciation for the hospitality extended to you. It is also customary to remove your shoes before entering someone's home, as a sign of respect for their property and cleanliness.

In social settings, such as restaurants and cafes, it is customary to greet others with a handshake and maintain eye contact during conversation. It is also polite to wait for the host or hostess to begin eating before you start your meal and to keep your hands visible on the table while dining.

When dining with Hungarians, it is important to observe proper table manners, such as keeping your elbows off the table, chewing with your mouth closed, and using utensils rather than your hands to eat. It is also customary to offer to pay for your share of the meal, although the host may insist on covering the bill as a gesture of hospitality.

In terms of social interactions, Hungarians tend to be more reserved and formal with strangers but warm and hospitable with friends and acquaintances. Personal space is valued, and it is polite to maintain a respectful distance from others during conversation. It is also customary to address people by their title and last name until given permission to use their first name.

Overall, navigating Hungarian etiquette and social customs requires a blend of respect, politeness, and cultural sensitivity. By observing these customs and showing appreciation for Hungarian culture, visitors can forge meaningful connections and create lasting memories in the beautiful and vibrant country of Hungary.

Folk Art and Crafts: Preserving Tradition in a Modern World

Hungarian folk art and crafts are vibrant expressions of the country's rich cultural heritage, reflecting centuries of tradition, craftsmanship, and creativity. From intricately embroidered textiles to exquisitely painted ceramics, Hungarian folk art encompasses a wide range of techniques and styles that have been passed down through generations.

One of the most iconic forms of Hungarian folk art is embroidery, which has been practiced in Hungary for centuries. Hungarian embroidery is characterized by its bold colors, geometric patterns, and intricate stitching techniques, which vary depending on the region and cultural influences. Traditional Hungarian embroidery often features motifs inspired by nature, such as flowers, leaves, and animals, as well as religious symbols and folkloric motifs.

Another beloved form of Hungarian folk art is pottery, which has a long and storied history in the country. Hungarian potters are known for their skillful use of clay and glazes to create beautiful and functional ceramic pieces, including plates, bowls, and vases. Traditional Hungarian pottery is often decorated with intricate patterns and motifs, such as floral designs, geometric shapes, and folkloric scenes, which are hand-painted or stamped onto the surface of the clay.

Wood carving is also an important aspect of Hungarian folk art, with artisans creating intricately carved sculptures, furniture, and decorative objects using traditional techniques and tools. Hungarian wood carvings often feature motifs inspired by nature and folklore, such as animals, mythical creatures, and symbolic motifs, which are carved into the surface of the wood with precision and skill.

In addition to embroidery, pottery, and wood carving, Hungarian folk art encompasses a wide range of other traditional crafts, including weaving, lace making, and leatherworking. These crafts are often practiced by skilled artisans in rural communities, where they are passed down from generation to generation as a way of preserving cultural heritage and supporting local economies.

Despite the challenges of the modern world, Hungarian folk art and crafts continue to thrive, with artisans finding new ways to adapt traditional techniques to contemporary tastes and markets. Many Hungarian artisans sell their work at local markets, festivals, and online platforms, where they attract both domestic and international buyers seeking unique and authentic handmade goods.

By preserving and promoting traditional folk art and crafts, Hungary honors its cultural heritage and ensures that these beautiful and meaningful traditions continue to inspire and delight people around the world for generations to come.

Hungarian Fashion and Design: A Blend of Tradition and Innovation

Hungarian fashion and design are vibrant and dynamic reflections of the country's unique cultural heritage and creative spirit. From traditional folk costumes to cutting-edge contemporary designs, Hungary's fashion scene encompasses a diverse range of styles, influences, and aesthetics that blend tradition with innovation.

One of the most iconic symbols of Hungarian fashion is the traditional folk costume, known as the "kalocsa," which originated in the Kalocsa region of Hungary. The kalocsa costume is characterized by its bright colors, intricate embroidery, and elaborate floral motifs, which are handcrafted with meticulous attention to detail. These traditional costumes are often worn during festivals, weddings, and other special occasions, serving as symbols of Hungarian identity and cultural pride.

In addition to traditional folk costumes, Hungary has a thriving contemporary fashion industry that is gaining recognition both domestically and internationally. Hungarian fashion designers are known for their innovative approach to design, drawing inspiration from a wide range of sources, including art, architecture, and pop culture. Many Hungarian designers have gained international acclaim for their bold and avant-garde designs, which push the boundaries of conventional fashion and challenge traditional notions of style.

Budapest, Hungary's vibrant capital city, is at the forefront of the country's fashion and design scene, with a thriving community of designers, artists, and creatives who are shaping the future of Hungarian fashion. The city is home to numerous boutiques, ateliers, and fashion events, where emerging designers showcase their latest collections and trends.

Hungarian fashion designers are also known for their commitment to sustainability and ethical practices, with many incorporating eco-friendly materials and production methods into their designs. This focus on sustainability reflects Hungary's broader cultural values of environmental stewardship and social responsibility, as well as the growing global movement towards more sustainable and ethical fashion practices.

In addition to fashion, Hungary is also known for its rich tradition of craftsmanship and design in other areas, including furniture, ceramics, and jewelry. Hungarian artisans are celebrated for their skillful use of materials and techniques, creating beautiful and functional objects that blend traditional craftsmanship with contemporary design sensibilities.

Overall, Hungarian fashion and design are vibrant expressions of the country's cultural identity and creative spirit, embodying a unique blend of tradition and innovation. Whether drawing inspiration from centuries-old folk traditions or pushing the boundaries of contemporary style, Hungarian designers continue to captivate and inspire audiences around the world with their creativity, craftsmanship, and artistic vision.

Sports and Recreation: From Football to Water Polo

Hungary has a rich and diverse sports culture that encompasses a wide range of activities, from traditional team sports like football and water polo to individual pursuits such as swimming and fencing. Sports play an integral role in Hungarian society, promoting physical fitness, teamwork, and national pride.

Football, or soccer as it's known in the United States, is the most popular sport in Hungary, with a long and storied history dating back to the late 19th century. Hungarian football clubs have achieved success both domestically and internationally, with teams like Ferencvárosi TC and MTK Budapest competing in European competitions and earning accolades on the global stage. The Hungarian national football team, known as the "Magyarok," has also enjoyed periods of success, including winning the Olympic gold medal in 1952 and finishing as runners-up in the FIFA World Cup in 1938 and 1954.

Water polo is another beloved sport in Hungary, with the country boasting a rich tradition of excellence in the sport. Hungarian water polo teams have consistently been among the best in the world, winning numerous Olympic medals and World Championships over the years. The Hungarian men's national water polo team, in particular, is considered

In addition to Budapest, Hungary's thermal spa culture extends to other regions of the country, including Hévíz, which is home to the largest thermal lake in Europe. The Hévíz Thermal Lake is fed by natural hot springs and is renowned for its healing properties, making it a popular destination for those seeking relief from arthritis, rheumatism, and other chronic conditions.

Hungary's thermal spa culture is not just about physical health; it also encompasses mental and emotional well-being. Many Hungarians view bathing in thermal waters as a form of relaxation and self-care, a chance to unwind and escape the stresses of daily life. Thermal baths often feature amenities such as saunas, steam rooms, and massage services, providing a holistic approach to health and wellness.

In recent years, Hungary's thermal spa culture has experienced a resurgence in popularity, with new spas and wellness resorts opening across the country. These modern facilities offer state-of-the-art amenities and services, while still honoring the centuries-old tradition of Hungarian thermal bathing.

Overall, Hungary's thermal spa culture is a testament to the country's commitment to health, wellness, and natural healing. Whether soaking in the mineral-rich waters of Budapest's historic baths or enjoying the tranquil surroundings of a thermal lake in the countryside, visitors to Hungary can experience the restorative power of Hungarian spa culture firsthand.

Transportation in Hungary: Navigating Roads, Rails, and Rivers

Transportation in Hungary offers a diverse array of options for navigating the country's roads, rails, and rivers, catering to both locals and visitors alike. The country's transportation infrastructure is well-developed and efficient, making it relatively easy to travel between cities and regions.

Road transportation is a popular choice for getting around Hungary, with a network of well-maintained highways, expressways, and local roads connecting major cities and towns. The road system is complemented by a comprehensive network of bus services, operated by both public and private companies, which provide convenient and affordable transportation to destinations across the country. Hungary's roadways are generally safe and well-marked, making driving a viable option for travelers who prefer the flexibility and freedom of having their own vehicle.

For longer-distance travel, Hungary's railway system offers a convenient and comfortable alternative to driving. The country's rail network is extensive, with frequent train services connecting major cities and towns throughout Hungary and beyond. Hungarian State Railways (MÁV) operates the majority of passenger train services in the country, offering a range of options from high-speed intercity trains to slower regional services. Traveling by train allows passengers to sit back, relax, and enjoy the scenic views of the Hungarian countryside while avoiding the stress of navigating traffic.

In addition to roads and rails, Hungary's extensive network of rivers and waterways provides another mode of transportation for both goods and passengers. The Danube River, Europe's second-longest river, flows through Hungary, serving as a vital transportation artery for cargo ships and river cruises. Hungary's capital city, Budapest, is situated on the banks of the Danube, and the river plays a central role in the city's transportation system, with passenger ferries and sightseeing boats offering scenic cruises along its historic waters.

In urban areas, public transportation options such as buses, trams, and metro systems provide efficient and reliable means of getting around. Budapest, in particular, boasts an extensive public transportation network, including a modern metro system, tram lines, and bus routes, which serve the city and its surrounding suburbs. The Budapest Metro, the oldest electrified underground railway system in mainland Europe, provides convenient access to key attractions and neighborhoods within the city.

Overall, Hungary offers a diverse and comprehensive transportation system that caters to the needs of travelers and residents alike. Whether traveling by road, rail, or river, navigating Hungary's transportation networks is a seamless and enjoyable experience, providing opportunities to explore the country's rich cultural heritage, natural beauty, and vibrant urban centers.

Economy and Industry: Hungary's Economic Landscape

Hungary's economy is a dynamic and diverse landscape that has undergone significant transformations since the fall of communism in 1989. Today, Hungary boasts a mixed economy with a strong emphasis on manufacturing, services, and innovation.

One of the key drivers of Hungary's economy is its manufacturing sector, which accounts for a significant portion of the country's GDP and exports. Hungary is home to a wide range of manufacturing industries, including automotive, electronics, pharmaceuticals, and machinery. The automotive sector, in particular, plays a crucial role in Hungary's economy, with multinational companies such as Audi, Mercedes-Benz, and BMW operating production facilities in the country. Hungary's strategic location in Central Europe, skilled workforce, and favorable business environment have made it an attractive destination for foreign investment in the manufacturing sector.

In addition to manufacturing, Hungary's service sector is also a major contributor to the country's economy, accounting for a significant portion of GDP and employment. The service sector encompasses a wide range of industries, including finance, tourism, telecommunications, and information technology. Budapest, Hungary's capital city, serves as the financial and commercial hub of the country, with a thriving business district and a growing number of multinational corporations and startups.

Hungary's agricultural sector, while not as prominent as manufacturing and services, remains an important part of the country's economy, particularly in rural areas. Hungary is known for its fertile farmland and diverse agricultural products, including grains, fruits, vegetables, and livestock. The government has implemented various policies and programs to support and modernize the agricultural sector, including subsidies for farmers, investments in infrastructure, and initiatives to promote sustainable farming practices.

In recent years, Hungary has also emerged as a leading destination for foreign direct investment (FDI), particularly in sectors such as renewable energy, biotechnology, and research and development. The Hungarian government has implemented a range of incentives and initiatives to attract foreign investors, including tax breaks, grants, and streamlined regulatory procedures. Hungary's strategic location within the European Union, well-educated workforce, and competitive business environment have positioned it as a key player in the global economy.

Despite its economic successes, Hungary faces various challenges, including income inequality, demographic decline, and structural reforms. The government continues to implement policies and initiatives aimed at addressing these challenges and promoting sustainable economic growth and development.

Overall, Hungary's economic landscape is characterized by diversity, innovation, and resilience, with the country's manufacturing, services, and agricultural sectors playing integral roles in driving growth and prosperity. As Hungary continues to navigate the complexities of the global economy, its commitment to innovation, entrepreneurship, and sustainable development will be key to ensuring a prosperous future for its citizens and businesses alike.

Environmental Concerns and Conservation Efforts

Environmental concerns and conservation efforts have become increasingly important topics in Hungary as the country grapples with various challenges related to pollution, habitat loss, and climate change. Hungary's diverse ecosystems, including forests, wetlands, and grasslands, are home to a rich array of plant and animal species, many of which are considered threatened or endangered.

One of the most pressing environmental concerns in Hungary is air and water pollution, particularly in urban areas where industrial activities and transportation contribute to high levels of pollutants. The government has implemented various regulations and initiatives to address air and water quality issues, including investing in cleaner technologies, promoting renewable energy sources, and improving wastewater treatment systems.

Another significant environmental challenge facing Hungary is deforestation and habitat loss, which threaten the country's biodiversity and natural landscapes. Hungary's forests are vital ecosystems that provide habitat for numerous species of plants and animals, as well as important ecosystem services such as carbon sequestration and soil erosion control. Conservation efforts are underway to protect and restore Hungary's forests, including reforestation projects, protected areas, and sustainable forest management practices. Wetlands are another critical component of Hungary's natural environment, providing important habitat for migratory birds, fish, and other wildlife. However, wetlands in Hungary are under threat from drainage, pollution, and development, leading to loss of biodiversity and degradation of ecosystem services. Efforts are being made to conserve and restore Hungary's wetlands through initiatives such as the Ramsar Convention on Wetlands and the European Union's Natura 2000 network.

Climate change poses a significant threat to Hungary's environment, with rising temperatures, changing precipitation patterns, and extreme weather events impacting ecosystems and communities across the country. Hungary is taking steps to mitigate and adapt to the effects of climate change, including reducing greenhouse gas emissions, increasing energy efficiency, and implementing climate resilience measures in infrastructure and land use planning.

Conservation organizations, NGOs, and grassroots initiatives play a vital role in addressing environmental concerns and promoting conservation efforts in Hungary. These groups work to raise awareness, engage communities, and advocate for policies and actions that protect Hungary's natural heritage and promote sustainable development.

Overall, environmental concerns and conservation efforts are central to Hungary's efforts to safeguard its natural resources, protect biodiversity, and ensure a healthy and sustainable environment for future generations. By addressing these challenges and working together to implement effective solutions, Hungary can continue to thrive while preserving its unique natural heritage.

Minority Cultures in Hungary: Preserving Diversity

Hungary is a country with a rich tapestry of cultural diversity, shaped by centuries of migration, conquest, and historical influences. Throughout its history, Hungary has been home to various minority groups, each contributing to the country's unique cultural mosaic. From the Roma people to ethnic Germans, Slovaks, Romanians, and others, minority cultures in Hungary play a significant role in preserving diversity and enriching the nation's cultural heritage.

One of the largest minority groups in Hungary is the Roma community, also known as Romani people or Gypsies. The Roma have a distinct culture, language, and traditions that have been passed down through generations. Despite facing discrimination and social marginalization, the Roma have made significant contributions to Hungarian society, particularly in music, dance, and handicrafts. Efforts are underway to promote Roma cultural heritage and address issues such as poverty, unemployment, and educational disparities within the community.

Hungary is also home to significant populations of ethnic Germans, Slovaks, and Romanians, among other minority groups. These communities have preserved their unique languages, customs, and traditions over the centuries, adding to the country's cultural diversity. In recent years, there has been a renewed interest in celebrating and promoting the cultural heritage of these minority groups, with festivals, events, and educational programs aimed at raising awareness and fostering appreciation for their contributions to Hungarian society.

Religious minorities also play a role in Hungary's cultural landscape, with communities such as Jews, Muslims, and Christians of various denominations coexisting alongside the majority Catholic population. Hungary has a long history of religious tolerance and pluralism, dating back to the Middle Ages when different faiths lived side by side in relative harmony. Today, religious minorities in Hungary have the freedom to practice their faith openly, and the government recognizes and protects their rights under the law.

Language is another important aspect of minority cultures in Hungary, with communities such as the German-speaking Swabians and the Slovak-speaking Csángós preserving their linguistic heritage through schools, media, and cultural institutions. While Hungarian is the official language of the country, minority languages are also recognized and supported, particularly in regions where these communities are concentrated.

Overall, minority cultures in Hungary play a vital role in preserving diversity, promoting cultural exchange, and fostering social cohesion. By embracing and celebrating the contributions of all its citizens, Hungary can continue to thrive as a vibrant and inclusive society that values the richness of its cultural heritage.

Immigration and Diaspora: Hungarian Communities Around the World

Hungarians have a long history of migration and diaspora, with communities of Hungarian descent scattered around the world. The Hungarian diaspora has been shaped by various factors, including historical events, economic opportunities, and political upheavals. One of the largest Hungarian diaspora communities is in the United States, where Hungarian immigrants have settled since the late 19th century. Many Hungarian Americans have preserved their cultural heritage through language, food, and traditions, contributing to the rich tapestry of American society.

In addition to the United States, significant Hungarian communities can be found in countries such as Canada, Australia, Argentina, Brazil, and Israel, among others. These diaspora communities maintain strong cultural ties to Hungary, organizing events, festivals, and cultural exchanges to celebrate their heritage and promote solidarity among fellow Hungarians abroad.

The Hungarian diaspora has also played a role in preserving and promoting the Hungarian language and culture outside of Hungary. Hungarian-language schools, churches, and cultural organizations serve as hubs of community life for diaspora communities, providing opportunities for language education, cultural enrichment, and social connection.

Historical events such as World War II and the Hungarian Revolution of 1956 have led to waves of Hungarian emigration, with many refugees fleeing political persecution and seeking asylum in countries around the world. These events have left a lasting impact on Hungarian diaspora communities, shaping their identities and influencing their relationships with their homeland.

Today, the Hungarian government recognizes the importance of the diaspora and works to support and engage with Hungarian communities abroad. The Office for National Policy for Hungarians Abroad (Nemzetpolitikai Államtitkárság) oversees initiatives aimed at strengthening ties with the diaspora, including cultural exchanges, language programs, and dual citizenship policies.

Despite the challenges of living far from their homeland, Hungarian diaspora communities remain connected to their roots and proud of their heritage. Through their efforts to preserve Hungarian culture, language, and traditions, diaspora communities contribute to the global spread of Hungarian identity and serve as ambassadors for their homeland on the international stage.

Government and Politics: Structure and Challenges

In Hungary, the government operates within a framework of a parliamentary democracy, with a multi-party system and separation of powers between the executive, legislative, and judicial branches. The Prime Minister serves as the head of government, while the President is the head of state, with mostly ceremonial duties. The Parliament, known as the Országgyűlés, is the country's legislative body, responsible for passing laws, approving budgets, and overseeing government actions.

Hungary has a unicameral parliamentary system, meaning it has only one legislative chamber. The Országgyűlés consists of 199 members who are elected to four-year terms through a mixed electoral system that combines proportional representation with a single-member district voting. Political parties play a significant role in Hungarian politics, with several parties representing diverse ideological and policy positions.

The dominant political party in Hungary is the Fidesz – Hungarian Civic Alliance, a center-right party led by Prime Minister Viktor Orbán. Fidesz has been in power since 2010, winning consecutive parliamentary elections and securing a supermajority in the Országgyűlés, which has enabled the party to implement significant reforms and policies.

One of the most controversial aspects of Hungarian politics in recent years has been the Orbán government's approach to democracy, rule of law, and human rights. Critics argue that the government has engaged in actions that undermine democratic institutions, restrict press freedom, and erode judicial independence. Hungary has faced criticism from the European Union and international organizations over these issues, leading to tensions between the Orbán government and the EU.

In addition to domestic challenges, Hungary also faces external pressures, including migration, regional security concerns, and economic integration within the European Union. The country's stance on migration, in particular, has been a divisive issue both domestically and internationally, with the government adopting a hardline approach and erecting border fences to prevent illegal crossings.

Despite these challenges, Hungary continues to be an active participant in international affairs, maintaining diplomatic relations with countries around the world and contributing to multinational organizations such as the United Nations, NATO, and the European Union. The country's geopolitical position in Central Europe gives it strategic importance in regional politics and security.

Overall, Hungary's government and political landscape are characterized by a complex interplay of institutional structures, party politics, and socio-economic factors. As the country navigates through its challenges and opportunities, the resilience of its democratic institutions and the engagement of its citizens will play crucial roles in shaping its future direction.

Hungarian Diplomacy: Navigating International Relations

Hungary, nestled in the heart of Europe, has a long history of diplomatic engagement on the international stage. As a member of various international organizations and alliances, Hungary plays a significant role in shaping global affairs and promoting its national interests. The country's diplomatic efforts are guided by a commitment to multilateralism, cooperation, and dialogue, as well as a pragmatic approach to advancing its strategic objectives.

One of the cornerstones of Hungarian diplomacy is its membership in the European Union (EU), which it joined in 2004 as part of the fifth enlargement of the EU. As an EU member state, Hungary participates in the decision-making processes of the European Council, the European Parliament, and other EU institutions, contributing to the formulation of common policies on issues such as trade, security, and migration.

Hungary is also a member of NATO (North Atlantic Treaty Organization), having joined the alliance in 1999. As a NATO member, Hungary is committed to collective defense and security cooperation with its allies, contributing troops to NATO missions and participating in joint military exercises and operations.

In addition to its membership in the EU and NATO, Hungary maintains diplomatic relations with countries around the world, pursuing bilateral partnerships and alliances to advance its economic, political, and security interests. The country's diplomatic network includes embassies, consulates, and other diplomatic missions in numerous countries, facilitating dialogue and cooperation on a wide range of issues.

Hungary's foreign policy priorities are shaped by its geopolitical position in Central Europe, as well as its historical, cultural, and economic ties with neighboring countries and regional powers. The country seeks to balance its relations with major powers such as the United States, Russia, and China, while also fostering closer ties with its Central European neighbors and partners in the Visegrád Group (Poland, Czech Republic, and Slovakia).

Hungary's diplomacy is characterized by pragmatism and flexibility, as it navigates complex international dynamics and seeks to advance its national interests in a rapidly changing global environment. Whether engaging in bilateral negotiations, participating in multilateral forums, or promoting cultural and economic exchanges, Hungary remains committed to diplomacy as a means of promoting peace, stability, and prosperity on the world stage.

Tourism in Hungary: Opportunities and Challenges

Tourism in Hungary is a vibrant and dynamic industry that attracts millions of visitors from around the world each year. From the historic streets of Budapest to the tranquil countryside and picturesque villages, Hungary offers a diverse range of attractions and experiences for travelers of all interests.

Budapest, the capital city, is a major tourist destination known for its stunning architecture, rich cultural heritage, and vibrant nightlife. Visitors flock to iconic landmarks such as the Buda Castle, the Parliament Building, and the Chain Bridge, which span the Danube River and offer breathtaking views of the city skyline. Budapest is also famous for its thermal baths, including the historic Széchenyi and Gellért Baths, where visitors can relax and rejuvenate in natural hot springs.

Outside of Budapest, Hungary boasts a wealth of natural beauty and cultural treasures waiting to be explored. The Danube Bend, a scenic stretch of the Danube River, is dotted with charming towns, historic castles, and vineyards, making it a popular destination for day trips and river cruises. The Lake Balaton region, often referred to as the "Hungarian Sea," is the largest lake in Central Europe and offers opportunities for swimming, sailing, and sunbathing along its sandy shores.

Hungary's countryside is dotted with picturesque villages, rolling hills, and vineyard-covered landscapes, providing a tranquil escape from the hustle and bustle of city life. Visitors can explore traditional folk culture and artisanal crafts in villages such as Hollókő, which is a UNESCO World Heritage Site known for its well-preserved architecture and rich cultural traditions.

The wine regions of Hungary, including Tokaj, Eger, and Villány, are also popular tourist destinations, offering wine tastings, cellar tours, and culinary experiences showcasing the country's rich viticultural heritage. Hungarian cuisine, known for its hearty flavors and diverse influences, is another draw for food enthusiasts, with traditional dishes such as goulash, lángos, and chimney cake delighting visitors' taste buds.

Despite its many attractions, Hungary faces challenges in the tourism industry, including infrastructure development, environmental sustainability, and competition from other destinations in Europe. The government and private sector are working to address these challenges by investing in infrastructure improvements, promoting sustainable tourism practices, and diversifying tourism offerings to attract a wider range of visitors.

Overall, tourism in Hungary presents both opportunities and challenges for the country's economy, culture, and environment. By capitalizing on its unique heritage and natural assets while addressing key challenges, Hungary can continue to thrive as a premier tourist destination in Europe, welcoming visitors from near and far to experience all that the country has to offer.

Cultural Exchange and Collaboration: Hungary on the Global Stage

Hungary's cultural exchange and collaboration efforts have played a significant role in shaping its global presence and fostering international understanding. The country's rich cultural heritage, combined with its strategic location in Central Europe, has positioned it as a hub for artistic, intellectual, and creative exchange on the global stage.

One of the primary avenues for cultural exchange is through Hungary's diplomatic missions abroad, which actively promote Hungarian culture and facilitate cultural exchange programs with other countries. These initiatives include art exhibitions, music performances, film screenings, and literary events that showcase Hungary's diverse artistic talents and cultural traditions to international audiences.

Hungary also participates in numerous international cultural festivals, biennials, and exhibitions, where Hungarian artists, musicians, writers, and performers have the opportunity to showcase their work and engage with their counterparts from around the world. These events not only promote Hungarian culture but also facilitate cross-cultural dialogue and collaboration, fostering mutual understanding and appreciation among nations.

In addition to traditional forms of cultural expression, Hungary is also actively engaged in promoting its intangible cultural heritage, including folk music, dance, craftsmanship, and culinary traditions.

Organizations such as the Hungarian Heritage House (Néprajzi Múzeum) and the Hungarian Cultural Institute (Magyar Kulturális Intézet) work to preserve, promote, and transmit Hungary's cultural heritage to future generations, both at home and abroad.

Hungary's cultural diplomacy efforts extend beyond the arts and humanities to include education, science, and innovation. The country's universities and research institutions collaborate with international partners on academic exchanges, joint research projects, and scientific cooperation programs, contributing to the global advancement of knowledge and innovation.

Hungary's membership in international organizations such as UNESCO (United Nations Educational, Scientific and Cultural Organization) and the Council of Europe further enhances its cultural exchange and collaboration efforts, providing platforms for dialogue, cooperation, and shared cultural heritage preservation on a global scale.

Through its commitment to cultural exchange and collaboration, Hungary continues to strengthen its ties with the international community, promote its cultural identity and heritage, and contribute to the enrichment of global cultural diversity and understanding. As the world becomes increasingly interconnected, Hungary's role as a cultural ambassador on the global stage remains vital in fostering peace, dialogue, and cooperation among nations.

Future Prospects: Challenges and Opportunities for Hungary

As Hungary looks to the future, it faces a mix of challenges and opportunities that will shape its trajectory in the years to come. One of the key challenges is economic inequality, with disparities between urban and rural areas, as well as social groups. Addressing these disparities will require targeted policies to promote inclusive growth and reduce poverty and social exclusion.

Another challenge is demographic change, with an aging population and declining birth rates posing long-term implications for the labor market, healthcare system, and pension system. Hungary's government has implemented various measures to encourage family formation and support working parents, but sustained efforts will be needed to address the demographic challenge effectively.

Hungary also faces environmental challenges, including air and water pollution, deforestation, and loss of biodiversity. Climate change poses additional risks, with extreme weather events becoming more frequent and severe. The government has introduced initiatives to promote renewable energy and sustainable development, but more ambitious action will be needed to mitigate the impacts of climate change and protect the environment for future generations.

On the economic front, Hungary has made significant strides in recent years, with strong GDP growth, low unemployment, and foreign direct investment driving economic expansion. However, the country remains vulnerable to external shocks, such as changes in global economic conditions or geopolitical tensions in the region. Strengthening resilience and diversifying the economy will be crucial for ensuring long-term prosperity.

Hungary's geopolitical position in Central Europe presents both opportunities and challenges. As a member of the European Union and NATO, Hungary benefits from access to European markets and security cooperation with its allies. At the same time, the country must navigate complex geopolitical dynamics, including tensions with neighboring countries and divergent interests within the EU.

Technological innovation and digital transformation offer opportunities for Hungary to enhance productivity, competitiveness, and quality of life. The government has prioritized investments in digital infrastructure, research and development, and education to capitalize on these opportunities and position Hungary as a leader in the digital economy.

Cultural diplomacy and soft power can also be leveraged to promote Hungary's interests and values on the global stage. Building on its rich cultural heritage and intellectual tradition, Hungary can strengthen its ties with other countries, foster mutual understanding, and enhance its influence in international affairs.

Overall, Hungary's future prospects will be shaped by its ability to address internal challenges, capitalize on external opportunities, and adapt to evolving global trends. By pursuing inclusive and sustainable development strategies, investing in human capital and innovation, and fostering cooperation with international partners, Hungary can chart a course toward a prosperous and resilient future.

Epilogue

In this journey through the vibrant tapestry of Hungary's history, culture, and society, we've delved deep into the heart of a nation rich in tradition, innovation, and resilience. From the ancient origins of its people to the challenges and opportunities of the modern era, Hungary's story is one of remarkable diversity and enduring spirit.

As we reflect on the chapters that have unfolded, we see a country shaped by centuries of conquests, revolutions, and transformations. From the glory days of the medieval Kingdom of Hungary to the tumultuous periods of Ottoman rule and Habsburg influence, Hungary has weathered storms of change while preserving its unique identity and heritage.

Through the turbulence of the 20th century, Hungary experienced the trials of two world wars, the upheaval of communism, and the struggles for independence and democracy. Yet, amid these challenges, the spirit of the Hungarian people endured, driving forward progress and renewal in the post-communist era.

Today, Hungary stands at a crossroads, facing both familiar obstacles and new horizons. Economic growth and development have brought prosperity to many, yet inequalities persist, and environmental concerns loom large on the horizon. The country's geopolitical position in Central Europe presents both opportunities for cooperation and challenges of navigating complex regional dynamics.

Yet, amidst these uncertainties, Hungary remains a beacon of cultural richness and intellectual vitality. Its vibrant arts scene, thriving culinary traditions, and dynamic cultural exchanges continue to captivate and inspire both locals and visitors alike. From the grandeur of Budapest's historic architecture to the tranquility of its countryside, Hungary offers a wealth of experiences waiting to be explored.

Looking to the future, Hungary's prospects are bright, fueled by a spirit of innovation, entrepreneurship, and global engagement. As the country charts its course forward, it will draw upon its rich legacy of resilience and adaptability to embrace the opportunities and challenges of the 21st century.

In this epilogue, we bid farewell to our exploration of Hungary, but our journey through its history, culture, and society will continue to inspire and enlighten us. As we part ways with this captivating land, may its stories and lessons linger in our minds, reminding us of the enduring spirit and timeless allure of Hungary.

Printed in Great Britain
by Amazon

46626902R00066